THE GARDENS OF
VENICE

THE GARDENS OF
VENICE

RIZZOLI
NEW YORK

PHOTOGRAPHS
BY
ALESSANDRO
ALBRIZZI

TEXT
BY
MARY JANE POOL

INTRODUCTION
BY
ILEANA
CHIAPPINI DI SORIO

ACKNOWLEDGMENTS

Many have encouraged us in the preparation of this book and we want to thank each of them. Some have opened the doors of their gardens, others the archives of their museums. Some have given us the benefit of their scholarly knowledge, others their professional experience.

Landscape architect Bruce Kelly has been a great source of consultation on plant species and historical references.

We were welcomed to the gardens of Mr. Alessandro Barnabò, Count Brando Brandolini d'Adda, Mrs. Carla Brass, Countess Cecilia Giustiniani-Recanati, Mrs. Evelina Levi-Broglio, Mr. Franco Lombardi, Countess Maria Lucheschi Czarnocki, Mrs. Liselotte Manera Höhs, Mr. Carlo Maria Rocca, Mr. Max Rocca, Count Giulio Rocca, Constance and Natale Rusconi, Mr. James B. Sherwood, the heirs of Count Trento's estate, and Count Giovanni Volpi di Misurata.

Needed permissions were given to us, or archives opened to us by: Professor Giovanni Castellani, Rettore Magnifico of the University of Venice; Dr. Franca Tiepolo, Director of the Archives of the City of Venice; Dr. Gian Domenico Romanelli, Director of the Museums of Venice; Professor Pietro Zampetti of the University of Urbino; Doctor Giovanni Busetto, Querini-Stampalia Foundation; Monsignor Giuliano Bertoli, Rettore of the Seminary of Venice; Monsignor Antonio Niero, Curator of the Patriarchal Museum; Dr. Attilia Dorigato, Curator of the Murano Glass Museum; Father Gabriele De Zan, Superior of the Convent of San Francesco della Vigna; Father Rafaello Andonian, Director of the Armenian College; Leopoldo Tonello of the Giorgio Cini Foundation; Dr. Philip Rylands, Deputy Director of the Peggy Guggenheim Foundation; Dr. Pier Paolo Pinelli, Secretary General of the I.R.E. of Venice; Urbano Pasquon, Riccardo Monni, and Umberto Lo Cascio of the Correr Museum; and James Draper, Curator of European Sculpture at the Metropolitan Museum of Art.

Others who have been most helpful: Ambassador Gerard Gaussens, Architect Riccardo Gaggia, Carola de.P. Kittredge, Marinella Herion, Countess Kenta Alverà, Countess Lesa Marcello, Donatella and Paolo Asta, Nicolò Asta, and Giorgio Reis.

And, we particularly thank Claudia McNulty, Bettina McNulty, and Jaye Holme for their research in London and New York.

We are greatly indebted to our publisher, Gianfranco Monacelli, who responded so quickly to the idea of the book, and to our editor, Robert Janjigian, who so expertly guided the book to completion.

Many more have assisted us in various ways during the four years of planning, researching, photographing, writing, and producing this book. We are most grateful to everyone who has expressed interest in the project, which has spurred us on, and to all who have given of their time to help us compile and publish the material found in these pages.

Scores of artists, architects, writers, scholars, and many visitors to Venice have left us the gift of their impressions of the gardens through the centuries. Their works have been a great source of information and inspiration to us, and we dedicate this book to them.

A.A., M.J.P.

First published in the United States of America in 1989 by
RIZZOLI INTERNATIONAL PUBLICATIONS, INC.
300 Park Avenue South, New York, NY 10017

Library of Congress Cataloging-in-Publication Data
Albrizzi, Alessandro.
   The gardens of Venice.
   Includes bibliographical references.
   1. Gardens—Italy—Venice—History.   2. Gardens—
Italy—Venice—Pictorial works.   3. Venice (Italy)—
Description—1981-   —Views.   I. Pool, Mary Jane.
II. Title.
SB466.I83V43   1989   712'.0945   89-45426
ISBN 0-8478-1121-2

Designed by Mary Jane Pool and Miki Denhof
Composition by David E. Seham Associates, Metuchen, NJ
Map by T.R. Lundquist
Printed by Dai Nippon, Tokyo, Japan

Front cover: *Courtyard of the palazzi Mocenigo*
Back cover: *Palazzo Giustiniani Recanati*
Endpapers, page 1: *Angel, Palazzo Giustiniani Brandolini garden*
Pages 2–3: *San Giorgio Maggiore cloister*
Pages 4–5: *Entrance to Palazzo Giustiniani Brandolini*
Pages 6–7: *Garden of Casa Rocca*
Pages 8–9: *Garden of Casa Rusconi*
Pages 10–11: *Garden of Casa Rocca*
Frontispiece: *Garden gate of Palazzo Albrizzi*
Page 14: *Courtyard, Palazzo Contarini Corfù dagli Scrigni Rocca*
Page 16: *Entrance to Palazzo Soranzo Van Axel*

CONTENTS

INTRODUCTION
BY ILEANA CHIAPPINI DI SORIO

Venice is an island city that owes its survival entirely to man's ingeniousness in taming the natural environment. Land is therefore a precious commodity. Perhaps as a consequence, few Italians take greater pleasure in flowers and gardens than these island dwellers, who seldom own more than a few feet of ground, and tenaciously cultivate every inch of soil within these narrow bounds.

Those gardens, sprinkled among the noble buildings, reveal an intensely urbanized people nonetheless determined to enjoy the pleasures of nature, who insist that their outdoor life be as fruitful and varied as that of a person who owns acre upon acre of land. The unique urban character of Venice is accentuated in these pockets of greenery.

Originally, Venice consisted of a number of small settlements on the various islands that comprise the city, connected by the network of canals that gave the area its indelible imprint—the *forma urbis* that is still visible today. A fifteenth-century schematic representation of the city, drawn by Jacopo de' Barbari and published by the merchant Antonio Kolb of Nuremberg, provides the earliest documentation of what the entire Venetian landscape must have looked like at the time of first settlement.[1] In the drawing, the shores of the outer reaches of the city—the southern edge of the Giudecca and its counterpart to the north—are largely barren, with a sparse covering of brush. This land had to be levelled and defended against erosion before it could be inhabited.

The first fences were erected to delineate land ownership, but the idea of the garden as an extension of the house or as a decorative complement to

The island of Guidecca, from a c.1500 engraving by Jacopo de'Barbari. Collection Correr Museum. Photograph courtesy of the Correr Museum.

it had not yet developed. The first cultivation was necessarily utilitarian in nature. Nevertheless, the *Barba Chronicle* reports that Doge Domenico Michiel erected a palace with a *zardin*, or garden, at San Giovanni in Bragora even before his election in 1118. The *Chronicle* notes that the Doge "many a time went to find amusement" in his garden—a recognition of the pleasure of leisure intellectual pursuit.

Glass and lattimo *garden centerpiece, designed in Murano, eighteenth century. Collection A. Rubin de Cervin Albrizzi, Venice. Photograph courtesy of Alessandro Albrizzi.*

1. G. Mazzariol and T. Pignatti, La pianta prospettica di Venezia del 1500, disegnata da Jacopo de' Barbari (Venice: Cassa di Risparmio, 1963); J. Schulz, "The Printed Plan and Panoramic Views of Venice," Atti e memorie di storia dell'arte (Venice: Fondazione G. Cini, 1970).

This is the earliest recorded mention of a garden in Venetian history. The Doge retired to the palace in 1129;[2] his garden, though still an anomaly, anticipated the importance of the concept of *delizia*, delight, in garden design.

Early in the thirteenth century, the Serenissima Republic granted permission to a Venetian doctor and scientist named Gualtieri to plant a botanical garden on the island of Sant' Elena, in order to raise herbs necessary for his practice and experiments.[3] Next to Gualtieri's stately stone house lay the "exposed area"; though a necessary adjunct to his practice, the garden probably lacked the social dignity that was to be attached to gardens in later eras. Gualtieri's garden was most likely just a courtyard, paved with a few bricks or flagstones: marble was too precious a commodity for building.

F. Colonna, Hypnerotomachia Poliphili, Venice, *engraving, 1499. Collection Correr Museum. Photograph courtesy of the Correr Museum.*

Throughout the history of Venice, the façades of buildings, rather than any natural landmarks, have been the primary determinants of the landscape. The will of the ninth-century Doge Giustiniano Partecipazio attests to the fact that buildings were often constructed of materials salvaged from earlier structures, particularly when those materials involved rich marbles or sculptured reliefs. Salvaged materials also came from the mainland, from the ruins of ancient towns, or from faraway lands, transported across the sea by traders. Upon attaining prosperity, these merchant seamen raced to embellish their formerly humble abodes with highly ornamented façades that in time became a familiar part of the cityscape. At one point, the Republic commanded sea captains to load not only goods, but also a certain quota of *esuvie*, the decorative stone slabs used for construction, in order to create a more spectacularly beautiful townscape.[4]

Informed by mandates such as this, it is no wonder that fifteenth-century Venice came to be called *la città picta*, "the painted city," for the brightly frescoed façades of its palaces, which were embellished with marbles and colorful architectural detailing. One might imagine that, alongside this development of the possibilities inherent in the private house, gardens would have assumed complementary importance. But the configuration of the city, with buildings clinging to every possible islet and rise in the ground, did not allow for expansive natural expression. Moreover, lacking as it is in natural vistas, the city's flat and somewhat dispiriting landscape tended to discourage a creative synthesis between landscape and traditional architecture.

One is left to guess at how Venetians in early centuries chose to organize the small outdoor spaces that existed on their properties. The de' Barbari map repeatedly reports the presence of square courtyards, hemmed in by crenelated walls. A raised well, set in a geometric pattern of stone or brick, was the central feature of the space. The perimeter walls were topped with a wide ledge which, once planted, served as an espalier or trellis. These courtyards traced their origins to the monastery cloister, although such a prototype might seem better adapted to the life of contemplation than that of the courtier. The paving over what in the monastery would have been a central orchard irrevocably obscured the symbolic relationship between this space and the late-Gothic conception of Paradise.

A small door in the perimeter wall led to the *brolo*, a term derived from the Celtic *bróghilos*, referring to an enclosed plot of land with an orchard. The de' Barbari plan identifies a number of *broli*, situated

2. Cronaca Barba (Barba Chronicle), *Venice: Marciana Library, Cod. Ms. It. LXVI = 76, carta 30 verso; see also G. Tassini, Curiosità Veneziane, 1970 ed. (Venice: Cecchini, 1863), p. 54.*

3. G. Damerini, *I giardini di Venezia (Bologna: Zanichelli, 1927), p. 36.*

4. S. Bettini, *Venezia e Bisanzio (Venice: Electa, 1974), p. 37.*

behind private houses or adjoining monasteries. The *broli* were often planted with fruits, vegetables, and vines. The vines would be trained to form a barrel-vaulted canopy that ran along a central axis leading to the edge of the water, calling to mind examples reported in Masuccio Salernitano's *Novellino*,[5] or the rose bowers and jasmine arbors that Colonna designed for his *Polifilo*. These trellised "hanging gardens" not only bore fruit but provided a shady retreat for walks (hence their characteristic vaulted shape). This shape was especially prevalent in the *broli* adjoining monasteries and on the island of Giudecca, which at the time was primarily a spot for summer houses.

With the building boom of the fifteenth century and the consequent development of open space for

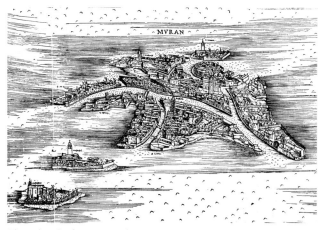

The island of Murano, from a c.1500 engraving by Jacopo de'Barbari. Collection Correr Museum. Photograph courtesy of the Correr Museum.

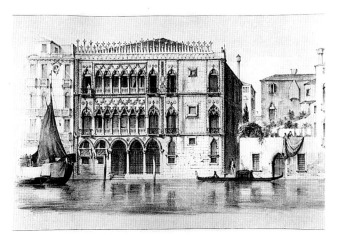

M. Moro, The Ca' d'Oro, Venice, engraving, nineteenth century. Collection Correr Museum. Photograph courtesy of the Correr Museum.

housing, these more homely gardens had to give way to an aesthetic better suited to the emerging class of merchant-patricians. One of the most characteristic fifteenth-century palaces is Ca' Contarini, usually called the Ca' d'Oro, or Golden House. Marino Contarini purchased the original structure from the Zeno family of S. Sofia in 1512, with the intention of erecting a refined and glorious abode. In order to design the residence, Contarini engaged renowned architects including Matteo Raverti of Milan and the Venetians Giovanni and Bartolomeo Bon. The French painter Giovanni Charlier, called "Zuan de Franza," enlivened the whorls and tracery of the façade, already rich in polychromed marble, with gold.[6]

A small but well-proportioned garden was placed between the two wings of the house and its crenelated side wall. It is difficult to imagine what

flowers and plants were grown there during the heyday of the Contarini, but if the gardens represented in fifteenth-century Flemish paintings can provide any clues, it probably attempted to create a microcosm of nature. There would have been the obligatory small rose bower, but the centerpiece of the garden would have been the carefully selected array of specimens of flowering plants so glowingly described by Cornelio Castaldi in verses about the Priuli garden.[7] Roses might have been accompanied by daffodils, violets, acanthus, and perhaps some cypresses, as depicted in the garden portrayed in the engravings of Jacopo da Varagine or the "Annunciation" by Carpaccio. The geometry of the garden would not have been as strictly imposed as that of the gardens of Cosimo il Vecchio in Florence, but a spoke-like arrangement of small pathways with the well at its hub was probably used in order to compartmentalize the flowers within it—an arrangement more in keeping with the concept of a secret garden, or garden within a garden, than with that of a formal park.

At the end of the fifteenth century, Casola described his astonishment at the beauty of the gardens on the island of Murano, and particularly "those near the religious houses of every order."[8]

5. Masuccio Salernitano, Il novellino (Venice: De Gregorii, 1492); P. Molmenti, La storia di Venezia nella vita privata, 7th ed. (Bergamo: Instituto Italiano Arti Grafiche, 1927–29. Reprint, Trieste: Lint, 1973), 2:181.

6. Molmenti, Venezia nella vita privata, 1:288; G. Lorenzetti, Venezia e il suo estuario, (Venice: Bestetti e Tuminelli, 1927. Reprint, Trieste: Lint, 1974), p. 423.

7. C. Castaldi, La villa Priuli in Murano, ed. by I. Bernardi, (Venice: Visentini, 1868), p. 147; Molmenti, Venezia nella vita privata, 2:198.

The de' Barbari map suggests that the monastery gardens were every bit the equal of those belonging to the private houses. Casola was also fascinated with the many boats moored at Murano, laden with fresh fruits and vegetables, such as lima beans, apricots, and cherries, in such quantities as to seem that "all the gardens in the world had been concentrated there." The produce gardens of the islands in the Venetian lagoon were quite celebrated. Andrea Calmo defined them as "veritable paradises on earth, the dwelling place of nymphs and gods."[9]

M. Moro, Palazzo Dario, Venice, engraving, nineteenth century. Photograph courtesy of Osvaldo Böhm, Venice.

In Venice proper, however, gardens still maintained the intimate character typical of the Gothic house. One surviving example is the garden of Palazzo Dario, which though no longer planted in the fifteenth-century manner is still interesting for the spatial relationships it reveals. The original Gothic structure was largely remodeled at the end of the fifteenth century: the façade overlooking the Grand Canal was covered with polychrome marbles in a style that has been described as "transposed Byzantine, framed within Renaissance stylistic elements."[10] The garden behind the house, surrounded by a crenelated wall, is raised slightly above the level of the ground floor in order to reinforce the impression that the visitor is entering a self contained microcosm of nature.

The garden of the Giustinian palace of San Barnaba, today called Brandolini d'Adda, is one of the few fifteenth-century details to have survived that house's subsequent modernization. Like the garden at Palazzo Dario, this rear garden is raised above the level of the rest of the house and is surrounded by a crenelated wall.

The Renaissance concept of landscape architecture, although eventually adopted throughout Italy, was slow to gain favor in Venice. Its more grandiose ideas had to be restrained to suit the exigencies of a city with no vast open spaces where grand schemes of architectonic symmetry could be imposed. Because of space limitations, Venetian landscaping never escaped its intimate character, even if it bowed in certain details to the fashion of the moment.

Historic and literary texts celebrate the Renaissance gardens of Venice, but these refer more often than not to the gardens of the outlying islands, in particular Murano and the Giudecca. The best known examples on Murano are the palazzi of the Mocenigo and Trevisan families. The Palladian-style palace of the latter may have been planned by Daniele Barbaro, the creator of the Botanical Gardens in Padua.[11] The building boasted frescoes by Prospero Bresciano; Alessandro Vittoria decorated the atrium leading to the garden with precious stucco designs. Paolo Veronese and Giambattista Zelotti contributed to the decoration of the rooms on the upper stories. The Cornaro palace, also on Murano, was home to Francesco Gonzaga in 1536. In 1553, one observer described the house's courtyards, loggias, grand staircases, and charming garden, "full of pleasant flowers, copious fruit and verdant grasses."[12] Gardens adjoining residences often included exotic plants grown for botanical study, as well as serving as meeting places for Venetian patricians and the noted artists and writers of the day.

8. P. Casola, Viaggio a Gerusalemme (Milan: Ripamonti 1855), pp. 9, 14; M.T. Boriosi-Cruciani, "Il giardino veneto," Antichità Viva, 5 no. 2 (1966): 41.

9. O. Lando, Sette libri di cataloghi e varie cose non solo antiche ma anche moderne (Venice: dé Ferrari, 1552), p. 490; Molmenti, Venezia nella vita privata: 2:198.

10. M. Marcello Grimani Giustinian, Palazzo Dario (Venice: Armenian Typography, 1985), p. 32.

11. M. Azzi Visontini, L'orto botanico di Padova (Milan: Polifilo 1984), p. 209.

12. G.F. Straparol da Caravaggio, Le piacevoli notti (Venice: G. Benadio, 1563. Reprint, ed. by G. Rua, Bari: Italy: Laterza, 1927), p. 6.

A more complete list of such gardens comes from Francesco Sansovino, whose famous father, Jacopo, created the plan of the Piazza San Marco, together with other notable projects that epitomize the townscape of Renaissance Venice. Sansovino exalts the many secret gardens that dot the city, including some too recent to be included on the de' Barbari map, as well as others on Murano and the Giudecca. He writes that notable gardens "of extraordinary ephemeral delicacy are scattered copiously" throughout the city. Their "variety of embellishments trimmed with green, including paintings, sculptured fountains, and other agreeable and graceful discoveries, give cause to rejoice to each one who looks at them, providing consolation and pleasure."[13]

Gardens in Venice, though obviously not as vast as those on the mainland, by this time had come to be seen as a natural complement to the house. Landscaping was treated as an architectonic element, complementing a highly ambitious and refined use of statuary and paintings, with themes dictated by literature. Sansovino lists several examples, some of great interest for his highly particularized description. He reports that Gaspare Erizzo embellished his palace garden at San Canciano with architectural motifs, sculptures, and celebrated paintings, later identified by Ridolfi as those of Paolo Veronese, who Erizzo's heirs commissioned to fresco the exterior walls of the palace. The frescoes facing the courtyard depicted ancient buildings and landscapes; those facing the canal, marine subjects. Martinioni in 1663 described the façade overlooking the garden as having loggias, sculptures, some by Alessandro Vittoria, and other Roman-style ornamentation.[14] These descriptions are an interesting reflection of prevailing tastes in Venice during the latter half of the sixteenth century.

The Erizzo palace appears in the de' Barbari map in its fifteenth-century incarnation, before it passed to the Morosini family. The latter were to become known as the family *dal giardin,* "of the garden," on account of the impressive park they later developed for the residence. The Morosinis enlarged the palace, thus enclosing the garden. In the mid-seventeenth century, the garden was replaced with a paved courtyard. The palace itself was eventually destroyed during the nineteenth century.

At the parish of San Trovaso, Sansovino writes that Pier Antonio Michiel planted some rare plants in a harmonious arrangement. Though he erroneously

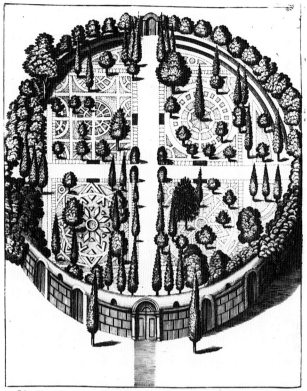

VIRIDARIVM GYMNASII PATAVINI MEDICVM.
Jo Georg sculps.

J. P. Tomasini, Viridarium gymnasii medicum, Udine, *engraving, 1654. Photograph courtesy M. Toso, Venice.*

called the proprietor by the name of Andrea, Sansovino accurately described the garden's glories. He writes of "important figures" in the garden, a possible reference to topiary. He also records a "beautiful fountain spouting sweet water," probably a throwback to the centrally placed well of the fifteenth-century garden.

Michiel's garden must have been remarkable not only for its highly formal arrangement but for his esoteric choice of plantings. The garden became famous for its herb and medicinal plant beds. At the time, the *tacuina sanitatis* spread the knowledge of the healing properties of such plants, previously the well-guarded secret of monasteries and herbaria that monopolized their cultivation. The sixteenth cen-

13. F. Sansovino, Venezia città nobilissima et singolare (Venice: D. Farri, 1581. Reprint, ed. by L. Moretti, Venice: Fillippi, 1968), pp. 369–70

14. C. Ridolfi, Le maraviglie dell'arte (Venice: Sgava, 1648. Reprint, Berlin: von Hadeln, 1914–21), p. 310; Sansovino, Venezia, pp. 369–70; E. Bassi, I palazzi di Venezia (Venice: Stamperia di Venezia, 1976), pp. 268, 273.

tury witnessed the growth of scientific interest in the study of medicinal plants. Amidst this scientific awakening throughout Europe, the Venetian Republic created the Botanical Gardens of Padua in 1545. The Paduan garden was considered a model scientific laboratory, due to its affiliation with the university there.[15]

An expert in botany, Michiel had written several tracts on plants and was in frequent contact with other scholars, such as Ulisse Aldovrandi of Bologna; Antonio Tolomei, who would send Michiel specimens from France; Fra' Taddeo, custodian of the garden of medicinal herbs at the monastery of San Cristoforo on Murano; and Andrea Pasqualigo, an expert in the cultivation of the castor-oil plant who maintained a garden at San Basilio, not far from Michiel's own at San Trovaso. Michiel's garden was considered a sort of botanical anthology, and experts frequently made long trips to visit it, as did Antonio Compagnoni da Macerata in 1554. Michiel's garden was cited for the rarity of its plants in Bauhin and Cherler's *Historia Plantarum Universalis* in 1651. Michiel was also in contact with traders from various countries, whom he identified in his notebooks as "itinerant herbalists," (most likely they were peddlers), and numerous amateur gardeners. He also maintained close relations with Venetian ambassadors and important merchants who could find him rare and exotic plant species from faraway lands. Among his many such contacts, Michiel was often in communication with the Fuggers of Augsburg, one of the great European mercantile families, whether directly or through their representatives in Venice.

In 1553, the Reformers of the Padua Studium, the governing body of the university, appointed Michiel superintendent of the Botanical Gardens. The university garden had been planned by Daniele Barbaro, and was built by Andrea Moroni.[16] The difficult choice of what herbs and other plants would be represented was entrusted to Luigi Squalerno, called *L'Anguillara*, after the name of his native village.[17] It is logical then to assume that the garden at San Trovaso reflected the same process of scientific selection employed in Padua. Mattioli praised the garden in 1568 for its *piante peregrine*, trailing plants, as well as for the feats of hydraulic engineering required to keep the central fountain supplied with water.[18] The garden was a clear product of the culture of the latter half of the sixteenth century, which favored a formal aesthetic based on scientific

research, nonetheless coupled with a penchant for the fantastic. A restless yet refined intellectual attitude, which might be called spiritual escapism, was typical.

On the spot of Michiel's garden today rises the Priuli-Clary palace. The present building bears little resemblance to the original structure on the site. Not far from it, hidden behind a wall, lies the garden of the sixteenth-century Trevisan-Giustinian Recanati palace. Although the garden's original layout has not been preserved, a "pictorial" quality is still evident in its tall forest trees, wisteria that grace the belvedere terrace, and the fountain that punctuates the

D. Dalle Greche, Mirto gentile lati folio (*myrtle in the shape of an eagle*), drawing, sixteenth century. Collection Biblioteca Marciana. Photograph courtesy of M. Toso, Venice.

grassy parterre. The perimeter walls are covered with creeping plants that further intensify the romantic intimacy of this spot, particularly in those moments when sunbeams filter through the foliage.

Cesare Ziliolo, chancellor to the doge, was linked to Michiel by his passion for botany. In his

15. M. Azzi-Visentini, L'orto botanico, p. 9; E. De Toni, "Notizie su Pietro Antonio Michiel e sul suo Codice-eario," Ateneo Veneto, 31, vol. 2, fasc. 1, July-Aug. 1908: 69–103; G. Targioni Tozzetti, Notizie della vita e delle opere di Pier Antonio Michiel (Florence: Le Monnier, 1868).

16. M. Azzi-Visentini, L'orto botanico, p. 152

17. Ibid., pp. 21, 106.

18. Ibid., p. 110, no. 11.

own garden near the Sant' Angelo church (unfortunately demolished in the nineteenth century), he had several examples of *ars topiaria*; a fountain, possibly with a marble bowl; and a large number of "rare plants brought from the Levant and new to this country."

Eager to give their garden a scientific veneer, the Grittis on the Giudecca undertook a similar venture, always careful however not to overshadow the aesthetic aspect of the enterprise. They realized their "delicate and rare" vision by scattering sculpture and architectural fragments among the evergreens, together with "pictures," presumably frescoes on the exterior walls of the manor house.

The diffusion of herb-growing in sixteenth-century gardens did not reflect a purely scientific interest, however: these plants may also have been incorporated into garden schemes because of their symbolic association with alchemy.

Gardens were by now inextricably linked with the daily life of the house, extending the living space and creating another pretext for entertaining guests. "Regular or periodic 'country' outings" took place, first in Murano, then throughout Venice. One particular brigade of pleasure-lovers was called the *zardinieri*,[19] "the gardeners," and met, appropriately enough, in one another's gardens, "anticipating the Venetian fashion for spending summers in the country."[20]

For centuries the *Casino degli Spiriti* has suffered a bad name owing to a misnomer: *spirito* in Italian means both "wit" and "ghost." It is in fact a small building on the lagoon facing the cemetery of San Michele, connected via a garden to the palace once belonging to Procurator Tommaso Contarini.

V. Coronelli, Cloister of San Giorgio, Venice, *engraving, seventeenth century. Collection Correr Museum. Photograph courtesy of the Correr Museum.*

The vast garden, once very famous, was mentioned in the 1663 edition of Sansovino and Martinoni's work, and was further documented during the eighteenth century when Francesco Guardi made a drawing and a painting of it.[21] The landscape architecture had meanwhile been altered to suit the malleability of taste of the period and the caducity of the vegetation, but part of the garden still surrounds the casino today. The term *casino* was often interchangeable with *ridotto*, or in Venetian *redutto*, from *redursi*, meaning "to get together," a word akin to the English redoubt, or meeting place. The first *redutto* in Venice dated back to 1282 and was located near San Basso, next to Piazza San Marco.[22] It was used exclusively by state officials, who after contentious sessions in the Doge's Palace would retire there to set aside their differences. By the sixteenth century the number of small buildings devoted to meetings and other intellectual pursuits had grown so large that every patrician family had more than one, although it is debatable whether their aims were always so lofty.[23] Nevertheless, in the sixteenth century, the Casino degli Spiriti was the meeting point of the "master-spirits" (hence its name) of the time, men such as Pietro Aretino, Sansovino, and Titian.

In 1549, Titian was living in a nearby house belonging to Bianca Pollani. He transformed the vacant plot of land next to his dwelling into a delightful garden which opened out onto the lagoon toward Murano, with a breathtaking view stretching unimpeded to the horizon.[24] The construction of the Fondamente Nuove embankment in the eighteenth century truncated Titian's garden and cut it off from its vista.

On the Giudecca, on the very tip facing San Giorgio Maggiore, Andrea Dandolo had a large house with a garden described as a "grand site, rich in lodges, courtyards, and loggias."[25] It was later

19. M. Sanudo, Diari by R. Fulin, F. Stefani, N. Barozzi, February 1514 (Venice: Visentini, 1879–1902).

20. Damerini, Giardini di Venezia, pp. 37, 43.

21. Sansovino, Venezia, p. 370. The painting is in the Rothermere Collection of the Ashmolean Museum, Oxford, UK.

22. G.B. Galliccioli, Delle memorie venete antiche (Venice: Fracasso, 1975), 1:831.

23. See also G. Dolcetti, Le bische e il gioco d'azzardo a Venezia (Venice: Manuzio, 1903), p. 234.

24. Damerini, Giardini di Venezia, p. 37.

25. Sansovino, Venezia, p. 369.

leased to a certain Marco Bragadino from Cyprus, also known as Momugna, who had arrived in Venice in 1590, and attracted some notoriety for his purported ability to turn mercury into gold. He furnished the palace with "rich and refined furnishings, while he himself was surrounded with a large number of servants who waited on him at banquets . . . with music and dances." The adventurer managed to get some money by dubious means but was soon chased to Padua by his creditors; from there he sought refuge in Bavaria, where he eventually died. During the seventeenth century the palace passed into the hands of the Nani family; Boschini records that the main façade was frescoed with the labors of Hercules by Paolo Veronese.[26] The house and its garden can be identified on the de' Barbari map: the property is adjacent to the monastery of St. John the Baptist, which later passed into the hands of the State as a consequence of Napoleon's edicts. On the southern side, beyond the garden wall, the map shows an empty plot of land extending toward the lagoon. In a 1566 engraving by Paolo Forlani, printed a few years later, the site appears walled and cultivated. A 1696 xylograph by Giovanni Merlo shows the former Dandolo estate in greater detail; its area is larger and a belvedere stands at the edge of the lagoon. Later engravings revert to the original boundary lines. Engravings by Coronelli and Lovisa in the eighteenth century indicate that the palace was still part of the holdings of the Nani family, and the seat of an academy.

The fall of the Republic witnessed a lamentable change in the use of the building: the gardens were replanted with vegetables, and the palace irreparably damaged. Today, only the gateway on the *fondamenta* remains; "the grand site with courtyards and loggias" has been lost forever. The site is now occupied by the Hotel Cipriani, the grounds of which still encompass, if in an altered state, part of the famous garden.

The house shown next to the Dandolo-Nani palace on the de' Barbari plan is in all likelihood the Vendramin residence: its courtyard and central well-head are clearly visible on the map. The present-day Calle Cavalerizza, which occupies the site of a former private riding-ground and stable, separates this house from succeeding structures, including the Palazzo Mocenigo. Alvise I, Tomà's son, had purchased this house and garden on the Giudecca at the behest of his wife Loredana Marcello, an expert botanist.[27] When her husband was posted to Padua,

Loredana took advantage of the opportunity to study with Melchiorre Guilandino,[28] the new resident professor at the famous Botanical Gardens there in 1564.[29] Pier Antonio Michiel dedicated his precious

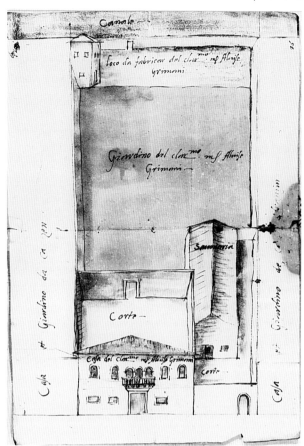

Plan of the Alvise Grimani house on the Guidecca, sixteenth century. Collection State Archives of Venice, Grimani Archive. Photograph courtesy of the State Archives of Venice.

herbarium, a five-volume treatise with drawings by Domenico Dalle Greche, to this doge's wife and accomplished botanist. The work today resides in the Marciana Library.[30]

Alvise Mocenigo learned of his election as doge in 1570 while he was in the Giudecca house. His reign was marked by several difficult moments:

26. M. Boschini, La carta del navegar pittoresco (Venice: BABA, 1660. Reprint, ed. by A. Pallucchini, Venice-Rome: Ist. per la collaborazione culturale, Fond. G. Cini, 1966).

27. Venice State Archive, Notarile, Testamenti (Last Wills and Testaments), B. 1256, no. 12.

28. A. Da Mosto, I dogi di Venezia (Milan: Martello, 1960), p. 278.

29. M. Azzi-Visentini, L'orto botanico, p. 106.

30. Ibid., p. 112; P.A. Michiel, I cinque libri delle piante, with drawings by Domenico dalle Greche, Venice: Marciana Library, Cod. Ms. It. II XXVI-XXX = 4860–4864.

in 1574 a fire ravaged the Doge's Palace, and the next year plague broke out in the city. That same year, however, Henry III, King of Poland, arrived in Venice on his way to Paris to receive the crown of France. The monarch was received with great ceremony by Doge Mocenigo and housed'in the Palazzo Michiel, overlooking the Rio della Sensa, a splendid palace which Sansovino mentions, among other reasons, for its frescos by Schiavone. Its garden, now lost, extended all the way to the Rio della Madonna dell'Orto.[31] A similar fate awaited the celebrated Foscarini gardens at the Carmini, where Henry of France was received when he came to Venice. In his honor, the Foscarinis had organized a *guerra dei bastoni,* a popular competition between opposing teams armed with clubs, in the square facing the palace.

An unpublished sixteenth-century drawing shows the plan of the Giudecca house of Alvise Grimani. The house had a walled courtyard with a door leading to the garden. Unfortunately, the garden is not described in any detail, although the area appears quite vast. The commercial activities of a *savoneria,* a nearby soap manufacturing plant, are given a much more prominent place in the record, to the exclusion of any description of the exact location of the Grimani property.[32] It is clear from the drawing that the house lay between the Zen and

F. Bertelli, Henri III received at the Lido, *engraving from a painting by A. Vicentino, sixteenth century. Collection Correr Museum. Photograph courtesy of the Correr Museum.*

Vendramin estates, although the latter is almost certainly not the Casa Vendramin, which was next to the Dandolo-Nani Palace on the de' Barbari map.

In 1589, in the parish of Sant' Eufemia on the Giudecca, Pietro Pasqualigo bought at auction a vineyard bordering one of his properties. The document of sale describes the vineyard as "under the open sky and planted with different trees," which it goes on to identify as various species of fruit tree. The vineyard was subsequently rented to Pasqualigo Negri; by this time the property had a small brick house, as well as sheds and outbuildings necessary to vine-growing. Further mention of the vineyard appears in a 1644 deed of sale when Vincenzo Pasqualigo, Pietro's son, sold it to Abbot Marino Zorzi; the deed records that the small brick house then rented for 70 ducats a year.[33]

From the description it is evident that the prop-

31. M.L. Richert, Ambasciatori di Francia (Verona: Triton Press, 1987), p. 16. © Associazione Culturale Italo-Francese, Venice.

32. Venice State Archive, Grimani Archives, B. 1.

33. Venice State Archive, Pasqualigo Archives, B. 1, March 20, 1589; Nov. 12, 1593; Feb. 7, 1644.

erty was valued primarily for the rental income derived from its use as agricultural land, very different from the Romanizing aspirations of the vineyard created by Vignola for the Villa Caprarola in 1559.

The island of the Lido, the outermost bulkhead of the Venetian lagoon against the forces of the Adriatic, was not as celebrated as Murano or the Giudecca: it boasted no frescoed houses, nor elaborate gardens enriched with rare species. The island had long played an important military role, however: its headlands overlooking the sea were fortified, and on its south side the forts of San Nicoletto and Sant' Andrea stood sentinel over the port entrance to Venice. Nevertheless, the heyday of the Lido began only during the 1850s, with its development as a fashionable seaside resort.[34]

Next to the San Nicoletto fort stood an eponymous church, where the doge, amid great pomp, would receive the city's most illustrious guests aboard the *bucintoro*, a ceremonial barge.[35] This pageant was frequently depicted by famous artists.

To the south, the island was capped by the port of Malamocco Nuovo, called "new" to distinguish it from the ancient Metamaucus of Roman origin, where the ducal government had established its earliest seat between 742 and 811, after Heraclea had been abandoned and before the definitive transfer of the capital to the island of Rivus Alto (Rialto), the site of present-day Venice. In 1106, a terrifying tidal wave swept away the old port, and in 1159 the new port was built on a more protected site to the west.

The interior of the island had a decidedly agricultural character; fruit, vegetables, and vines were grown there.

In 1573, the governor of the hospital of San Lazzaro dei Mendicanti granted the Venetian nobleman Daniele Pisani dal Banco the perpetual use of a vineyard with a *domo de muro*, or brick house, located on the Lido at Quattro Cantoni for an annual payment of 40 ducats. The area, now called "Quattro Fontane," was, during the sixteenth century, the narrowest part of the island. Pisani began work on his vineyard at once, probably in emulation of Cardinal Grimani, who had a very famous vineyard in Rome.

No record remains, but it stands to reason that the property included not only vines and fruit trees, but perhaps also a country house and summer lodge. Sixteenth-century Venice could no longer accommodate large agricultural areas, and land was becoming scarce on the nearby islands of the la-

goon as well. A vineyard along the lines of the Roman model was by this time only possible outside the city.

The sack of Rome in 1527 led illustrious artists including Pietro Aretino and Jacopo Sansovino to seek refuge in Venice, where they were attracted by an emerging pro-papal sentiment among the patrician families and the availability of lucrative commissions for their mannerist works. These artists were instrumental in introducing the taste and culture of Central Italy to Venice.

Perhaps with this new sensibility in mind, the Pisanis conceived of their vineyard as a place of intellectual pastimes and gatherings, of course without neglecting the opportunity to engage in a profitable commercial activity. An unpublished ledger has been discovered in which all expenses incurred from 1573 to early 1575 were meticulously entered. The fact that large sums were expended on stones, roof tiles, mortar, and lime; on the wages of masons, carpenters, canaldiggers, and other laborers; and on the fees of the *proti*, or architects, seems to confirm that the vineyard also included a notable architectural effort, most likely a casino or garden pavillion. It is likely that the casino was surrounded by open arcades on its four sides: an entry under "stone masons" dated June 26, 1574, allotted 454.5 Venetian lire "to buy the flagstones for the loggias in the vineyard building." Other entries include the retainer paid to Zuan Antonio Rusconi, a well-known architect and treatise-writer, for the construction of two stairways in Rovigo stone (June 24, 1573), and a payment to Francesco Muraro, ("mason"), for installing two chimney hoods in the casino on July 17,

---

34. *The earliest recorded episode of public bathing on the Lido dates back to the eighteenth century. Because a Venetian girl was involved the incident created quite a sensation, and the Inquisition, a particular magistracy of the Venetian Republic, began an investigation. The report by Gianbattista Manuzzi found that bathing was frequent on Sundays, Mondays, and Thursdays. Because no patricians took part in the activity, however, the Inquisitors dropped the matter altogether. R. Gallo, "Il Lido spiaggia balneare nel '700," Ateneo Veneto, 127, No. 5–6, May–June 1940: 150–520. In the mid-nineteenth century the first commercial bathing establishment on the Lido was promoted by entrepreneur Giovanni Busetto Fisola. By 1857, the Lido was equipped with "royal baths" reserved for members of the royal family who wanted to take advantage of the beneficial effects of sea-bathing. See G. Pecorai, Appunti per una storia del Lido (Venice-Lido: Atiesse, 1983); G.D. Romanelli, Le Venezie possibili (Milan: Electa, 1985), pp. 182–83.*

35. *The Bucintoro was the Ducal barge, used for outings in the lagoon on official occasions. The word derives from burchio d'oro, "golden boat." The Bucintoro was in fact adorned with gilded wood carvings.*

1574 (entry under "stonemason"). Zuane Marangon was engaged to lay "le volte," the wooden ceilings, (January 31, 1574, under marangoni, or carpenters). On September 4 the barge carrying the graici, the wattles to which the ceiling plaster was applied, reached the Lido (entry under "conveyance").

The ledger specifies each worker's professional qualifications, but does little to shed any light on the division of labor among them, a regrettable omission given the participation of a number of illustrious architects on the project. It is known that between July and August 1573, a total of 244 lire and six soldi were paid to the proti, and that Gian Antonio Rusconi submitted three designs for the casino, receiving for them in total a fee of 77 lire. Rusconi himself directed the early stages of the work, and together with Andrea Fisara actually laid the foundations. The latter was in charge of hydraulic engineering and had drawn up a "plan for the waters of the embankment of the vineyard," leading one to gather that at least one side of the estate bordered upon a canal. Today Fisara could be described as an urban planner: in addition to his other duties, he was also responsible for laying out the roads within the property. Presumably no roads existed in that rural area and everything had to be built anew. Even Antonio da Ponte, the designer of the Rialto bridge, was called upon in his official capacity as proto alle acque, the architect of the office overseeing the protection of the lagoon, to define the boundaries of the property. Paulo da Ponte, probably a relative, was responsible for drawing up the map for the title registry and overseeing the masons' work.

On April 19, 1573, the name of Andrea Palladio is mentioned several times, but no specific task is assigned to him. Presumably he had been commissioned to design the decorative parts of the casino, because one of the entries in the ledger records a payment of eight lire to him for "the shapes of the capitals," suggesting the existence of a colonnade. Palladio appeared in the ledger again on October 25 of the following year, when "he advised that the ceiling vaults should be built under Master Zuane." Palladio was evidently supervising the work alongside Master Zuane, who could only be Giovanni Antonio Rusconi, the architect who had plannned the building. The last entry concerning Palladio is dated April 23, 1575, when his fees were settled.

A more modest structure had evidently been demolished to make room for the casino: the ledger records that "five days' pay went to a stonemason for demolition of the old structure." There is mention also of a small stable for "the mares" (November 7, 1573, under "works"). The final cost of the entire job was 276,624.15 Lire, of which Palladio's fees, like Rusconi's, amounted only to 77 lire. Temanza (1762) had surely seen the building when he stated that the plan was by Rusconi and not by Palladio, to whom the project had often been attributed. He added that although Palladio had often been consulted, this was not enough to make him the architect of the building.

The inclination of contemporary observers to assign the Pisani casino to Palladio suggests how Palladian in style it must have appeared. Rusconi undoubtedly felt the influence of his eminent colleague with whom he had collaborated on various projects, including the interiors of the Ducal Palace, after they were consumed by fire in 1574.[36]

The Pisani vineyard is the only documented sixteenth-century architectural undertaking on the Lido. Still closely connected to agricultural pursuits, it was nonetheless meant as a place of rustic delights, after the fashion prevalent on the mainland. Other vineyards existed on the island but their purposes were wholly different.[37] The subsequent history of the property as traced through surviving documents is interesting and complex. In 1706, the value of the property was estimated to be 4,600 ducats, of which the annual rental payment of 42 ducats was still owed to the Hospital of San Lazzaro dei Mendicanti. The lease passed to Girolamo Pisani dal Banco and Chiara Pisani Moretta upon their marriage in 1721, and to the latter alone when she was widowed in 1738. Meanwhile, in 1729, the estate was rented to Gian Maria Moretta, in no way related to the Pisani Moretta family of San Polo, and the building underwent a restoration at a cost of 1,389.12 ducats. In 1750, the lease on the vineyard passed for 15 years to Antonio Pasini, reverting in 1776 to Zuanne and Iseppo Moretta, who quite likely were related to the preceding tenants. Iseppo still held the tenancy in 1801.

In 1750, Giovanni Filippini, Chiara Pisani Moretta's personal architect, was entrusted with another

36. Venice: Correr Museum, Lazzara Pisani Zusto Archives, B. 49, file 7. See also T. Temanza, Vita di A. Palladio (Venice: Pasquali, 1762), p. 57.

37. Venice State Archive, Misc. Maps 15, Mar. 18, 1766, negative D 5 24/16, positive 17. Another vineyard, owned by a Lunardo Malipiero, is reported in 1766 without further details.

extensive and costly restoration for 4,000 ducats. He drew a map of the property, now lost but still available in 1820 when litigation broke out over the boundaries. Under the decision that resulted in 1836, 1,088 square meters were sold to the Direction of Fortifications of the Imperial Crown of Austria in order to construct a seafront fort. This fort, the Quattro Fontane, was demolished in the early part of this century.

Contemporary sources report even more detailed information. In 1818, the estate was still 5.3.117 Paduan fields in area, with a manor house and several outbuildings. The neighborhood was now called Quattro Cantoni, bordered on one side by the beach where the fort was erected and on the opposite side by the lagoon. The other two sides of the property bordered on vineyards, former religious properties that had been expropriated by edict of Napoleon in 1806 and sold at auction. A further document dated May 14, 1835, issued by the Municipal Congregation, recognizes a refund of 635 lire paid annually to Chiara Pisani Barbarigo for wages she paid to Giovanni Goattin, the keeper of the four "tanks." These were four large natural reservoirs of rainwater, situated near the shoreline a few meters beneath her property, which since time immemorial had been reserved for public use. The present-day neighborhood of the Quattro Fontane, or four fountains, owes the name, through a bit of poetic license, to the presence of these reservoirs.

Pietro Vittore Pisani, Chiara Barbarigo's stepbrother, came into possession of the vineyard but sold it in 1847. Attached to the deed of sale is a drawing that depicts the Quattro Fontane fort and indicates the boundaries of the estate. Taken together with a map of the Lido dated circa 1870 and an 1876 map made by engineer Emilio Pallesina, the Pisani property is easily identifiable with the area located between the Casino, which like the Palazzo del Cinema was built on the foundations of the old fort, and the modern Hotel Quattro Fontane. Final evidence is offered by comparison of the lot numbers on the title register.

One more map, drawn up when the streets on Lido were relaid between 1905 and 1909, indicates that the Pisani house was still quite imposing, with two lateral wings, probably loggias, as evidenced in a drawing contained in the Pisani archives. The names of the owners had changed, but the structure that Palladio had worked on probably survived until the early years of the twentieth century virtually un-

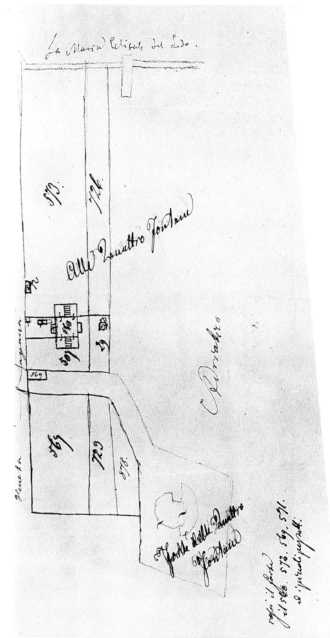

Plan of the Pisani vineyard, Lido, 1909. Collection Correr Museum, Lazara Pisani Zusto Archives. Photograph courtesy of Giacomelli, Venice.

scathed. The heavy hand of urban renewal in the 1930s finally obliterated any remaining traces of the old Pisani vineyard. The four "tanks" still visible in the 1876 map were capped or incorporated into other works: one into the fort and one into the building of the Marine Hospital. The remaining two were buried beneath newly paved streets.[38]

The early seventeenth century witnessed a growing interest in citrus trees, which had just been introduced to the region. Significant in this regard is the contract for the Genoese landscape gardener Gio Batta Cavazza, dated December 1611, who was hired to tend the orangery in the Montegalda Castle, near Vicenza. The castle was built around the remains of a Roman tower, which was fortified in 1176, and since that time has maintained its exterior aspect intact. The castle was built on a *motta*, or medieval earthenwork mound, and, owing to its particularly strategic position was fiercely contested by the lords of Verona and Vicenza and the Venetian Republic. In 1455, it fell into Venetian hands, and the Serenissima Republic donated it to the Chiericati family of Vicenza, who one century later sold it to the Venetian Andrea Contarini. Contarini willed the castle to his daughter Piuchebella, the wife of Nicolò Donà. Donà undertook its transformation into a patrician manor, adding gardens beyond the ramparts and a greenhouse along the medieval curtain wall. The contract recites Cavazza's qualifications not only as a gardener but as an *inzegniero*, or architect/ engineer, and his resumé stresses his professional experience acquired during journeys to Spain and Sicily. He was charged with "pruning the citron, lemon, and orange trees, all the espaliers and rose bushes, the fruit-trees and every other sort of plant, jasmine flower, and tree." An addendum to the contract specifies the inventory of tools entrusted to Cavazza. He was to remain in Contarini-Dona's service

for the rest of his life, even bequeathing to his lady all of his worldly possessions.[39]

The *Sommarione della Mappa*, the Land Book of the Comune of Montegalda, records that in 1810 the castle and garden were still part of the Donà estate; they later passed to the Grimanis, and then to the Marcellos following a marriage between these two Venetian clans. In 1971, the castle was ravaged by a fire that broke out in the west wing and was in danger of collapse. Thanks to Luciano Sorlini's providential purchase, the castle has now been painstakingly restored, the old *cedrera*, or orangery, revived, and a new terraced garden planted on two levels, thus taking advantage of the downward slope. The landscaping faithfully follows the eighteenth-century scheme with closely cropped parterres, subdivided with geometric precision and all lines converging at the center.

A garden in Biron, in the countryside near Vicenza, also bears the signature of a great architect, Francesco Muttoni. Muttoni designed the garden at the turn of the eighteenth century for the Zileri dal Verme family, while Giambattista Tiepolo was decorating the villa's walls and ceilings with frescoes. The new taste for wooded groves had begun to infiltrate this otherwise eighteenth-century arrangement: carefully chosen rare trees stand side by side with ancient cedars of Lebanon (perhaps brought to Vicenza by the villa's owner), and carob and loquat trees.

The eighteenth-century ideal of the monumental villa set in equally monumental grounds reached its apotheosis in the Pisani villa at Strà, near Padua, Gerolamo Frigimelica's theatrical elaboration of a modest existing structure into a manor for Alvise Pisani, Procurator of St. Mark. Its full splendor is recorded in the engravings of Giovan Francesco Costa, printed in the mid-1700s, which show the *parterres de broderie* in the garden behind the

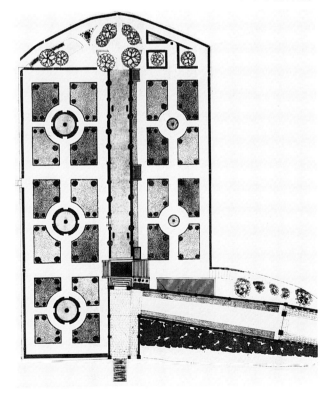

Plan of the gardens of the Montegalda castle near Vicenza, twentieth century. Collection Mr. L. Sorlini, Venice. Photograph courtesy of Mr. L. Sorlini.

38. For information regarding the transfers, see G. Gullino "I Pisani dal Banco e Moretta," Italia Europa (Rome: Istituto Storico Italiano, 1984), pp. 431, 437. Research on the sixteenth century in the Venice State Archive produced no result, and no mention of the episode exists in the records of the Water Magistrate. E. Corti, Lido di Venezia (Venice: Ferrari, 1919). The plan is in the Correr Museum, Lazzari Pisani Archives, B. 49, and in the Municipal Archives of Venice, Files 9/1/31 and 9/1/8. See also P. Paleocapa, Sulla costituzione geologica del bacino di Venezia (Venice: Cecchini, 1844); L'acquedetto di Venezia (Venice: Marsilio, 1984), p. 20.

39. G. Perbellini, "Il castello di Montegalda, da motta medioevale a villa veneta," Castellum, no. 24, 1984, 121. Venice State Archive, Donà, Private Archive, B. 42, Cavazza File.

house. Those flower beds have long disappeared, but the hillock, dotted with thickly wooded clumps, the belvedere, Guarini's labyrinth, the lemon grove, and the monumental stables still remain impressive to the modern visitor. The grand conception of this prestigious architectural complex, now the property of the State, has been splendidly preserved.

Abbot Martinioni, who revised and enlarged Sansovino's work, provides a further source of information on Venetian gardens.[40] He describes as notable the Grimani garden in the parish of S. Marcuola, which overlooks the Grand Canal and contains cypresses and various plants and flowers in patterned arrangements. The palace was purchased in 1589 by Vettor Calergi. Calergi bequeathed it in his will to his daughter Marina,[41] who married Vincenzo Grimani in 1608. In 1614, Marina had the wing of the palace planned by Vincenzo Scamozzi enlarged and a garden added. Though Marina left her entire estate to her three sons in a will dated 1634, they proved to be such scoundrels that the Republic confiscated all of their property in 1658. The Scamozzi wing was razed to the ground and a column of infamy erected on the site as a reminder of the atrocious crimes—unfortunately unspecified—committed there. Two years later, however, the brothers obtained a pardon; they were able to recover their entire estate and promptly rebuilt the demolished wing in the form in which one sees it today. The palace owes its present-day name of Vendramin-Calergi to a later marriage.

M. Moro, Palazzo Vendramin-Calergi, Venice, *engraving, nineteenth century. Photograph courtesy of Osvaldo Böhm, Venice.*

The palace of the Sangiovantoffettis, a rich family from Cremona who were enrolled as patricians in 1649, had a garden which is mentioned but not described by Ridolfi.[42] The palace had originally been built for the Marcellos and later belonged to the Foscarinis. Tintoretto executed the fresco paintings of the façade with themes from Ovid's *Fables.* Although the boundaries of the garden are still intact, it has not retained its original design, and today has the aspect of an English country garden. Surrounding the palace are other gardens, once part of the estate of the San Trovaso Church, which were expropriated and auctioned off by edict of Napoleon.

In 1604, Canon Stringa supplemented an edition of Sansovino's *Venezia città nobilissima* with his *Addenda,* the descriptions in which reveal just how architecturally elaborate contemporary gardens had become. Stringa describes how upon entering the house of Santo Cattaneo, on the Giudecca near the Convertite Monastery:

One first enters a square room, around which there is a colonnaded corridor as if in theatre, decorated with fresco paintings on the vaulted ceiling and in the perspective friezes. . . . From this room one passes into a courtyard with grottoes and fountains formed with sea stones, sponge-like and naturally hued, and multicolored ash solidified in the Murano furnaces; the stones are artfully arranged in a pattern, some heaped in mounds and some partly buried, and then studded with seashells, coral, sculpture, and other ornament of indescribable beauty. Water gushes out in all directions through the many underground jets that spurt water upward in thin streams through small holes bored into the floor, which is paved with square bricks. . . . Often those walking about . . . suddenly feel that the soles of their feet and their breeches are wet.

Signor Cattaneo had obviously bowed to the current fashion for bizarre garden scenography, in clear contrast to the geometric order and rigor that had guided Renaissance plans. Fortunately, on the Giudecca he had a fair amount of space at his disposal; a similar scheme could not have worked in the center of the city, where all available land had already been developed and the relationships between buildings and open space remained fixed. The courtyard evoked a fantastic undersea world,

40. Sansovino, *Venezia,* p. 369.

41. Venice State Archive, *Notarile Testamenti (Last Wills and Testaments),* B. 1261, no. 891. See also G. Mariacher, *Il palazzo Vendramin Calergi* (Venice: City of Venice, 1965).

42. Ridolfi, *Maraviglie dell'arte,* p. 310.

with mysterious coral- and shell-encrusted ridges and grottoes formed from sea stones and ashes from the glass furnaces of Murano—all materials that had been specially ordered during the planning phase of the project. Waterfalls and waterworks completed the effect, one obviously inspired by late-mannerist Medici gardens such as the one at Pratolino, where Buontalenti had assisted the hand of Nature with artificial grottoes and waterworks.

The courtyard gave onto a garden proper, one of extreme length which was probably subdivided in a geometric arrangement by pathways extending almost to the edge of the lagoon. A large frescoed loggia, with corridors and small communicating rooms facing the water, enjoyed a panoramic view beginning with the garden and extending as far as Malamocco and Chioggia. Such a view was entirely consonant with the Renaissance concept of the landscape-subordinated garden (in this case, seascape-subordinated). Stringa's description closes on a note of almost excessive enthusiasm: he writes that in that "spacious and delightful house, one could enjoy the best of both worlds: sea and mountains, woods and forests, and all that could enhance the mind and lift the spirits."[43]

The plants grown there were "noble and rare": Stringa mentions orange and citron trees, which presupposes the existence of hothouses for the winter; jasmine, espaliered to ornament the loggias and walls; and *fiori pellegrini*, medicinal herbs and flowers cultivated for their therapeutic value in imitation of the Renaissance tradition.

Cardinal Giovanni Dolfin, Patriarch of Aquileia, bought this enchanting locale for 1,000 ducats from Cattaneo's widow, Angela, shortly after Cattaneo's death in 1671. The deed of sale defines the property simply as a house with *"horto e altre fabbriche,"* a garden and outbuildings, the latter probably referring to the loggias built in front of the lagoon.[44]

Venice did not lack examples of roof gardens, although they were not common. Once again, they are mentioned in Stringa's book. The most remarkable specimen belonged to nobleman Simone Santo, secretary of the Republic, who created on the roof of his San Gregorio house a garden with "rare and precious plants; a mountain, a fountain, niches and other similar things that he built with his own hands; and mills and other waterworks, wonderful to behold for the abundance of water spouting from every side." A roof garden alone would have been

surprising enough without the addition of mills and a fountain, which must have made it downright odd. It is evident that contemporary taste strained for effect, substituting the understatement of the cloister, which typified earlier Venetian secret gardens, with opulent Baroque fantasies to which Venice is arguably unsuited. One explanation can be found in the intense theatrical activity of the period, which certainly must have influenced the aesthetics of decoration generally.

This is not to say that roof gardens were unknown in Venice. On the contrary, in their less excessive incarnations they posed one solution to the chronic lack of space. One such garden from the period still exists today: the fifteenth-century palace of the Contarinis della Porta di Ferro. This branch of the family took its name (*porta di ferro* means "iron gate") from the wrought-iron gate at their palace in the parish of San Francesco della Vigna. Upon entering the courtyard one is immediately struck by the original open staircase in Verona marble designed by Matteo Raverti from Milan, the same architect who worked on the plans for the Ca' d'Oro.[45] After the first flight of stairs, a side passageway marked by a Gothic portal leads to the roof garden, still highly evocative even though in a state of total abandon, its few haggard trees the only reminders of the "intellectual delights" of the fifteenth century.

By the beginning of the eighteenth century Venice, by now cut off from any active role in European politics, faced a future full of unknowns. Nevertheless, the formality and dignity born of a noble tradition die hard, particularly when one is still surrounded by all the trappings of apparent wealth. The city was still a magnet for persons of culture and cosmopolitan travelers on the Grand Tour. Artistic and intellectual life was at its apex, heralding new concepts and modern ideas. In particular, painters and sculptors of international fame revived the supremacy that the city had enjoyed during its "golden century."

The eighteenth century witnessed the unleasing of a frenzied quest for sumptuousness in music, drama, and the visual arts. Feasts, gambling, masquerades, theater-going, and intrigue became a

43. Sansovino-Stringa, Venetia città nobilissima et singolare (Venice: Altobello Salicato, 1604).

44. (Venice: Correr Museum, Ms. P.D. C.2500/X.

45. Molmenti, Venezia nella vita privata, 1:303.

way of life. Carnival was the culmination of this activity, an uninterrupted spectacle mixing the commemoration of particular episodes of Venetian history with non-stop revelry involving the whole population. For the 1768 carnival the Gradenigos even organized a bull hunt—part sport and part spectacle—in their garden near Rio Marin, opening it for the occasion to all comers.

This garden was the largest in Venice, having grown by gradually absorbing adjacent properties in a relatively out-of-the-way area of the city, at first with the sole utilitarian purpose of growing produce. In 1542, Bartolo Gradenigo had purchased a house with a quay on a canal that flowed into the Grand Canal near Sant' Agostino. Later, with a deed dated October 20, 1553, Gradenigo annexed another house whose boundaries reached from Rio Marin to the Calle delle Chiovere and the Church of San Simeone Piccolo (also called S. Simeone Apostolo).[46]

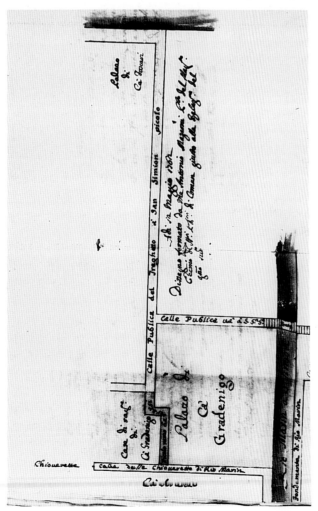

A. Mazzoni, plan for the enlargement of the Gradinego property, drawing, 1762. Collection State Archives of Venice. Photograph courtesy of the State Archives of Venice.

The family manor was reconstructed in the second half of the eighteenth century in accordance with plans by Domenico Margutti,[47] but surely at least part of the famous garden had been planted earlier if in 1748 there is mention of the existence of an orangery. The property was subsequently bisected by a public street, leading the Gradenigos in 1762 to petition the government to cede them the street for their private use. The concession was granted in 1764, and the Gradenigos proceeded to demolish the wall and modify the street. The result was an open space the size of about three Venetian fields, or 2.5 acres, stretching all the way to the Church of S. Simeone on the Grand Canal.[48] Such was the size of this garden that it contained a riding course and stables, and a carriage and four could be driven through it. Little remains of that wonder: between 1920 and 1921 it was subdivided and row houses for state railway workers built on the site.[49]

The Gradenigo estate bordered on the garden of Palazzo Soranzo, later Bragadin-Cappello, erected in the seventeenth century and celebrated for its interior decoration of marble.[50] The garden appears in an engraving by Vincenzo Coronelli, aligned along an axis that extends from the façade of the house. A short flight of steps flanked by two parterres connects the house to avenue, which itself was lined with a series of statues on pedestals. Statues of the twelve Caesars can still be seen along the perimeter walls. The decorative scheme was based on themes from Roman history, which were quite popular at the time, and included two sculpted groups depicting the rape of the Sabine women.

Another vast garden famous during the eighteenth century was that of the Savorgnans, a family from Friuli who had a palace near San Geremia with a façade by Giuseppe Sardi. In 1752, the garden was extended and adorned with ponds, marble statues, fruit and citrus trees, and evergreen hedges along the avenues. The garden inspired the poet Ni-

46. Venice State Archive, Gradenigo Private Archive, B. 41 bis, File 2–3.

47. Bassi, Palazzi di Venezia, p. 244.

48. Venice State Archive, Giudici a Petizion (Judiciary Petitions), Inventario di Gerolamo Gradenigo (Inventory of Gerolamo Gradenigo), Sept. 14, 1749, no. 23; Venice State Archive, Provveditori di Comun (Superintendency of the Commune), B. 52, and Senato Terra (Land Senate), 1723.

49. Tassini, Curiosità veneziane, p. 315.

50. Damerini, Giardini di Venezia, p. 42; Lorenzetti, Venezia e il suo estuario, p. 478.

candro Jasseo to write in Latin verses:

. . . The guest, admiring the whole Savorgnan house, lingers in the vast garden. The lovely bowers lead to the orchards: here the citrus branches hang low with fruit; the beautiful interweaving boughs form a barrel vault. In the house, the captive bird sings, and lonely freedom requires song.[51]

In 1826 the property passed to Baron Francesco Galvagna, who placed his collection of Roman inscriptions in the garden. Galvagna modified the landscaping with trompe-l'oeil perspectives, and in keeping with the Romantic taste of the period, had a small temple, a pagoda, and an Etruscan house erected in the groves.[52]

The garden presents quite a different face today, and shows traces of the influence of English-style landscaping, though this may be due more to neglect than any thought-out plan.

France played a dominant role in shaping Italian taste throughout the eighteenth century, and Venice was no exception. Guardi's drawing of the Contarini garden at Madonna dell'Orto illustrates this trend. The drawing depicts a fountain at the center and rectangular parterres—a detail not present in the actual garden—with curved shorter sides outlined by closely cropped borders. This geometrical arrangement is reminiscent of the gardens of Lenôtre, if on a more modest scale owing to the relative lack of variety in the landscape.

This garden served as the inspiration for the "shadowy garden" in poet Gabriele d'Annunzio's novel La Leda senza Cigno (1913). The description is of course a literary one, but seems to point to a new archeological consciousness, intent upon the rediscovery of the Italian-style garden, whose arrangement was closer to the poet's own sensibility than that of French models:

It is artfully built upon sixteenth-century vestiges, secretly architectural, similar to the ground-floor halls and chambers of a garden palace where a ladylike Season lives, refined but not averse to obscuring her mild grace with a certain carelessness.

Through her iron gates she gazes at the lagoon towards Murano and San Michele. . . .

She has her old walls, her ancient enclosure, where every morning she has lived her life, suffered her sorrows, seen the ghosts of bygone times resist or yield to the corrosion of centuries and salty air, enflamed or subdued her color.

. . . Her bowers are supported by old columns,

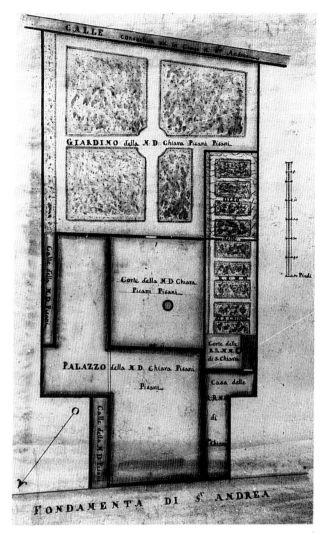

Plan of the palace and garden of Chiara Pisani Moretta at Santa Chiara, Venice, c. 1750. Collection State Archives of Venice. Photograph courtesy of the State Archives of Venice.

old capitals, old beams, where the boughs do not seem to find solace even upon bearing and shedding their flowers.[53]

In houses for rental, gardens, if present at all, were likely to have a very traditional layout which the tenant could change if he so desired. The plan of one of Chiara Pisani Moretta's houses, drawn around 1745–50, displays traditional Italian-style landscaping, devoid of all French influences: the parterres are plain and rectangular, with corners rounded only where they meet at the center around

51. Tassini, Curiosità veneziane, p. 582.

52. F. Gera, I principali giardini di Venezia (Venice: Antonelli, 1847), p. 13.

53. G. D'Annunzio, Il fuoco (Milan: Mondadori, 1942), pp. 1298–99.

the fountain or wellhead. The building and its garden stood in the area between the convent of Santa Chiara and the church of Sant' Andrea, both suppressed after the Napoleonic edicts of 1806.

In 1712, at the age of seventeen, Chiara Pisani Moretta married Gerolamo Pisani dal Banco, a distant relative of the San Stefano branch of the family. When she came into her late father's estate in 1739, she started an intensive and systematic renovation program, first of her palace at San Polo, calling eminent artists including Piazzetta, Angeli, and Tiepolo to decorate it, and then of the buildings she let for rent.[54] Her ledgers record all the payments to skilled workers for the restoration of the palace at S. Andrea. The plans are unsigned, but should probably be attributed to Giovanni Filippini, who from 1739 to 1770 was the architect of choice of the Pisani Moretta family. The whole area was altered in the 1930s to accommodate Piazzale Roma, and all traces of the garden vanished.

An unusual document was attached to the 1746 contract of sale for a *casino delle delizie* on the Giudecca, sold by Marc'Antonio Giustinian to Gerolamo Corner for 1,000 sequins (a Venetian gold coin).[55] Beyond the usual description of the house and its furnishings, the document contains an inventory of plants in the hothouses, and all the trees on the property. Unfortunately the list does not enumerate the garden plants or vegetables, an oversight rectified by Francesco Milliani, head gardener, who updated the list in 1749. One greenhouse contained 800 Flemish carnations, which were used for espaliers and the ornamentation of stairways. In addition, the garden contained an orangery with potted citron and sweet lemon trees, Portuguese orange, blood orange, pear trees, a grapefruit tree, "ungrafted" lemon trees, a large number of *bugarini* and *gimé*, (orange blossom), aloe plants,[56] rose bushes and trees, oleanders, a great profusion of jasmine: wild jasmine espaliered on the northern wall, the more delicate Spanish variety trellised onto the southern walls, as well as potted yellow jasmine. Along the perimeter walls there were boxwood hedges under which grew *flamboese*, or raspberries, and red currants. Fig trees and muscat grapevines were frequently trellised onto the walls of the house. Around the earth mound—which was a must for the conservation of any winter snow which might fall, and ice to be used to make sherbet—there was the orchard with white and red *lazzaroli* (a type of apple), various kinds of pear trees, plum trees called *zucchette im-*

periali and *zucchette bianche*, and almond trees.[57] About 50 cypresses formed the grove surrounding the belvedere, which probably overlooked the lagoon, as was the custom. Even the gooseberry bushes were espaliered to border the vegetable garden. The list reports many other fruit trees, among them a *zizoler* or jujube tree (*Ziziphus sativa*), the wood of which is used to make fifes. A poem by Pascoli mentions "a festive din of jujube fifes." An eighteenth-century scholar, Targione Tozzetti, observed that the jujube tree flowers late in spring but sheds its leaves very early in autumn, writing that "When the jujube tree covers itself [with flowers] you uncover yourself, when it uncovers itself you cover yourself."[58]

A final document of great relevance in this outline of eighteenth-century landscaping is an engraving by Luca Carlevaris, a landscape painter and protegé of the Zenobio family, depicting one of the three Zenobio gardens.

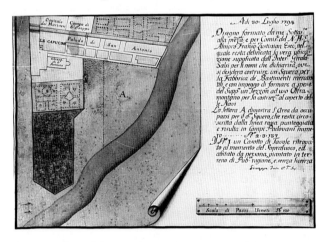

G. Foin, plan of the garden and monastery of the Sant'Antonio church, Venice, 1794. Collection State Archives of Venice. Photograph courtesy of the State Archives of Venice.

54. I. Chiappini di Sorio, Palazzo Pisani Moretta (Milan: Ricci, 1983), pp. 27, 30, 31, 39.

55. Venice: Correr Museum, Ms. P.D. C.2502/II.

56. Bugarini or mugherini (Sambac magorium) are sweet white flowers similar to orange blossom. Gimé (Sambac iasminum) is another species of fragrant white flower, imported to Europe from Goa in 1689. Lazzaroli is a fruit resembling apple, which grows on the azerole tree (Crataegus azarolus). Pereri fruttanti are fruit-bearing pear trees. Boerio, Dizionario del dialetto veneziano (Venice: Santini, 1829. Reprint, Milan: A. Martello, 1971). Piante d'aolè (Aloe succotrina) is the aloe plant, grown both for ornamental and medicinal purposes. G. Negri, Erbario figurato (Milan: Hoepli Milano, 1964), p. 49.

57. Zucchette imperiali and zucchette bianche are plums with a particular oval shape.

58. G. Targioni Tozzetti, quoted in C. Lunardi, "L'albero delle giuggiole," Gardenia, no. 29, September 1986, p. 130.

The Zenobios were an old Trentino family who moved to Venice and at the end of the seventeenth century bought a fourteenth-century palace located near the Carmini church. By 1700, the palace had been thoroughly restructured in accordance with plans by Antonio Gaspari. Two vast gardens surrounded the building, as witnessed by a 1783 map drawn by Girolamo and Pietro Soardi and today contained in the Albrizzi family archives.[59] The map makes clear the diversity of arrangement between the two gardens. The one nearer the palace had, before 1783, the original and unusual scheme visible in Carlevaris' engraving: a single parterre with a large mass of flowers at its center, hemmed by low hedges highlighting the delicate floral motif.

The arrangement of this garden, though deviating from the model created by Lenôtre in a few of its details, was nonetheless inspired by him. It is clear that the Zenobios had wanted a garden in the French style.

Tommaso Temanza designed a loggia meant to house a library and a study for the garden in 1767, thus noticeably altering its aspect. The loggia was described in 1841 as "a small recreational building by the celebrated architect Temanza, with a loggia and peristyles over which a terrace is placed in front of the library and the small rooms adjoining it."[60] Part of the garden still exists today, though the original plan is no longer recognizable.

The end was drawing near for the glorious and millenary Venetian Republic. After 1793, revolutionary winds were blowing across the Po Valley from France and a weak government led by the timorous doge Ludovico Manin was unable to oppose the rush of events. Without any resistance, in 1797, the curtain fell on the old Republic: in spite of a heroic but ineffective popular uprising, the flag of St. Mark was lowered and the new "democratic" republic under French control proclaimed. With the treaty of Presburg in 1805, Venice was annexed to the dominion of Napoleon Bonaparte, Emperor of France, who flattered the latent nationalistic spirit of the Italians by proclaiming a Kingdom of Italy under his control. It was to be a very short reign: the kingdom fell, together with Napoleon's fortunes, at Waterloo in 1814. Joachim Murat's defeat that year at Tolentino decreed the passage of the kingdom into Austrian rule.

Early in his reign, in 1806, Napoleon paid an official visit to Venice which he intended to commemorate by providing the city with an imposing

public garden with tree-lined promenades. The site chosen was called Motta di Sant' Antonio, in the Castello District, where an elongated public garden was to be connected with the Riva degli Schiavoni by filling in the canal called the Rio di Castello. The plan was part of a larger scheme concerning the suppression and confiscation of ecclesiastical es-

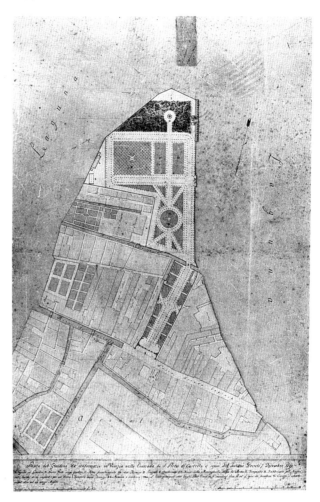

G. A. Selva, plan for the Napoleonic Gardens (Public Gardens), Venice, 1808. Collection Correr Museum. Photograph courtesy of the Correr Museum.

tates. The new public gardens were to rise on the area of the demolished churches and convents of San Domenico, S. Nicolò di Bari, Sant' Antonio Abate, the monastery of the Capuchin nuns, a seminary, and a seamen's hospital, plus the church and

59. Venice: A. Rubin de Cervin Albrizzi Archive, Reg. 39. The drawing of the Zenobio house is in the A. Rubin de Cervin Albrizzi Archive, B. 178/2.

60. Temanza, once the Zenobios' architect of choice, was replaced late in his life by Gerolamo Soardi and his son Pietro. Venice: A. Rubin de Cervin Albrizzi Archive, Reg. 39, "Dedication of the Architects."

convent of San Giuseppe, later spared and still standing today.[61] The architect appointed to plan the gardens was Gian Antonio Selva, well known for his design of the old La Fenice Theater (1790–92), destroyed by fire in 1836 and later rebuilt, and a triumphal arch erected over the Grand Canal for Napoleon's visit.

The plans for the gardens were exhibited in 1808 in the rooms of the renovated Academy of Fine Arts, housed in the former Carità church and convent. Selva had designed the main entrance on Via Eugenia (now Via Garibaldi), a large street built over the filled-in Rio di Castello in 1807. The plan called for five wrought-iron gates, arranged in a semicircle and giving onto a long, wide avenue, gently sloping downward, which would cross the San Giuseppe Canal and broaden out into the vast garden. Along the water's edge facing Sant' Elena there were to be steps where gondolas could be moored, while inside the park there would be tree-lined avenues, and thickets interspersed with kiosks and statues of mythological figures. A hillock would be created at the outermost tip of the site overlooking the lagoon, and a rotunda built to serve as a public meeting place.[62]

The project met with immediate public approval, but did not survive the detailed scrutiny of Viceroy Eugène Beauharnais. Selva finally modified the plans to accommodate the Viceroy's desire to reduce the financial outlay.[63]

The landscaping was entrused to a Venetian nobleman, Pier Antonio Zorzi, who as a man of letters and an expert grower possessed the same credentials that Pier Antonio Michiel had brought to bear on the Botanical Gardens in Padua. Zorzi decided to move into a small house on the grounds in order better to follow the work. The house is dilapidated but still exists, and is called by the name of "the gardener's cottage."

The Napoleonic Gardens were officially opened to the public in 1810 amid a chorus of praise.[64] One of the dissenting voices was the art historian and critic Pietro Selvatico. Disregarding the intentional simplicity of the plan, he pointed out that the avenues were monotonous and that the distribution of the groves inharmonious, lacking the picturesque quality of English-style gardens.[65] Selvatico could not countenance Selva's rigorous layout, evidently inspired by the style of the English landscaper Inigo Jones.[66]

In 1895, the gardens became the seat of the

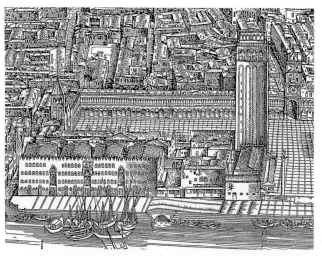

The granaries of the Republic of Venice in San Marco, from a c. 1500 engraving by Jacopo de' Barbari. Collection Correr Museum. Photograph courtesy of the Correr Museum.

International Exhibition of Modern Art. The mayor of Venice at the time happened to be Riccardo Selvatico, a descendant of Pietro, who modified the Napoleonic layout in order to construct pavillions for the exhibition.

In the temporary euphoria aroused by the Na-

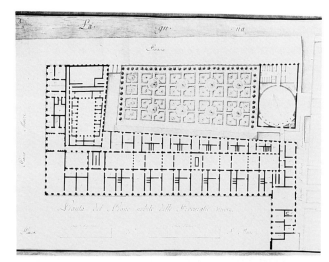

G. Antolini, plan of the piano nobile of the Procuratie Nuova, with garden on the site of old granaries, 1806. Collection Correr Museum. Photograph courtesy of the Correr Museum.

61. Damerini, Giardini di Venezia, pp. 5–7.

62. Ibid., p. 5.

63. G.D. Romanelli, Venezia nell'Ottocento (Milan: Electa, 1983), pp. 50–51; Romanelli, Venezie possibili, p. 158.

64. Romanelli, Venezia nell'Ottocento, p. 53.

65. P. Selvatico, Sull'architettura e sulla scultura in Venezia (Venice: Rigamonti-Carpano, 1847), pp. 474–75; Romanelli, Venezia nell'Ottocento, p. 121.

66. Romanelli, Venezia nell'Ottocento, p. 51.

poleonic projects, the negative dimension of arbitrary and indiscriminate demolitions was overlooked, and many artistic and historic monuments of great value were lost to the sledgehammer as a result. The most tragic loss was the Church of San Giminiano, razed to erect the Napoleonic wing closing Piazza San Marco. The old Granaries of the Republic, whose brick façade is clearly visible in the de' Barbari map, shared the same fate. The area cleared was used to create a garden for the royal residence at the time being constructed in the environs of the Procuratie Nuove in Piazza San Marco.

Private citizens sought to emulate the Napoleonic examples, and those patrician houses lacking a garden now strove to find room for one. Between 1815 and 1850, many wealthy Venetians had the small houses surrounding their palaces—and sometimes even other palaces—demolished, and gardens laid out in their stead.

One such example is the Albrizzi garden in Sant' Aponal Parish. The Albrizzis came from Bergamo, settling in Venice in the seventeenth century. They bought the first floor of the Bonomo palace in 1647, purchasing the rest of the building in 1692.[67]

Extensive renovation of the palace followed immediately. The portico was decorated with paintings connected to the ceiling and walls with a series

Visiting card of Countess Alba Albrizzi Zenobio, engraving, eighteenth century. Collection A. Rubin de Cervin Albrizzi, Venice.

of precious stucco moldings supported by angels, as if they were carrying framed pictures. In 1771, the Albrizzis acquired some small adjoining buildings which they thought defaced the façade of their palace and had them demolished, thus forming the present Campiello Albrizzi. They also created a garden opposite the house, spanning the canal with a

private bridge. The area they purchased in 1820 for the garden was the former site of the Tron di San Cassiano Theater. This theater, one of the oldest in Venice, had originally been opened to the public in 1636 by the Tron family who introduced the innovation of selling tickets to paying spectators. The theater reached the apex of its popularity in the eighteenth century with musical drama. The building had been restructured in 1763 by the architect Bognolo, but as the political situation deteriorated with the fall of the Republic in 1797 and the ensuing French domination, theater-going declined. Notwithstanding these setbacks, the theater kept its doors open until the early years of the nineteenth century, always under the ownership of the Trons.[68]

Eugenia Tron Veronese and her business partner, Santo Visetti, had the theater declared unsafe in 1810. In May of that year they obtained permission to demolish the theater and turn the site into a fruit and vegetable garden, on the condition that the area remain walled. The theater was in ruin but still standing ten years later when Alba Zenobio, Alessandro Albrizzi's widow, bought the site on March 8, 1820. On March 22 she was sued by Pietro Roggia, an actor who owned an adjoining property demanding the restoration of the walls which had been demolished due to the "insecurity" of the stone. A settlement was reached on June 13, with Roggia receiving 107.20 lire in compensation.[69]

Gian Antonio Selva has traditionally been identified as the landscaper of the garden, although the only evidence supporting this is his long professional association with the Albrizzi family. Selva, together with an engineer named Solaro, had carried out a survey and appraisal of the palace in 1804 when the Albrizzi estate was divided between Alessandro and his cousins Giuseppe and Vincenzo.[70]

A few years later, in 1833, a new architect, Gian Battista Meduna, came to sort out the longstanding contentions about the division of the estate. He was to enjoy the trust of the family for more than twenty years, and in 1857 prepared a statement of their assets which described both the gardens of the Preganziol villa and those of the palace in Venice.

67. Venice: A. Rubin de Cervin Albrizzi Archive, B. 1892, nos. 1–2.

68. N. Mangini, I teatri di Venezia (Milan: Mursia, 1974), pp 98–104.

69. Venice: A. Rubin de Cervin Albrizzi Archive, B. 182–4, no. 4, March 8–22; May 10–11.

70. Venice: Correr Museum, Dolcetti Bequest, File 4.

Meduna considered the garden of the Preganziol villa "grand and pleasurable, conducive to pleasant, contemplative walks." He underlined the importance of large, central avenues to its design, even though the landscape could, at least by comparison with English-style gardens, appear "monotonous" and "less indefinite" an imitation of "fair and picturesque nature" as a result. Despite the unfavorable comparison, Meduna praised the garden for its "majestic and refined aspect."[71]

Meduna's description, while strictly professional, betrays in its liberal use of adjectives an admiration for the garden of the villa which he lacked for the garden in Venice. His brief report on the latter reports that a bridge connected the first floor of the house with a small tower-like building containing a spiral staircase, through which one gained access to the garden. The grounds had tortuously winding footpaths bordered by vegetation, in spots forming a sort of canopy. As to the vegetation, Meduna remarked only that "various plants thrive there, mostly forest trees," suggesting that some time would be required before the garden attained full growth.[72] Very little space was given to flower beds; the tall evergreens so dear to English-style landscaping evidently prevailed. This detached and brief account tends to suggest that Meduna had no professional involvement with this garden, even though the architect who was responsible for it remains unknown.

Research in the Albrizzi family archives has yielded a relief map of the garden, drawn by Meduna in 1862; attached to it are two designs for wrought-iron grilles. The garden today still displays its original features, including a hillock that was created on top of the raised stage of the former theater. This spot affords a view of the canal, across the part of the garden occupying what used to be the orchestra seats. The garden was restored to its former scheme by architect Bruce Kelly in 1985.

Another site where smaller structures were demolished to make way for a more imposing garden is the Palazzo Cappello Malipiero at San Samuele. The house is a thirteenth-century building that was refurbished in 1622. Cattarin Malipiero originally owned only part of the house, brought to him as a dowry by his wife, Elisabetta Cappello. In 1620 he managed to acquire the whole building, a fact attested to in his will of 1631: "bought two-thirds of the ground floor of the house at San Samuele and the entire top floor, and I had the whole rebuilt." By so doing, Malipiero settled a boundary dispute with the Vendramin estate that had been dragging on since 1591.

The eighteenth-century engravings show a quay-side house with *bastion*, a wine-selling tavern, that stood on the area now occupied by the garden, and a wall separating the house from the Grand Canal. Access was gained through an alley running along the left-hand side of the palace; it was this easement that had provoked the litigation with the Vendramins.[73]

The palace was restored again in 1890, a fact recorded on a stone tablet found buried in the garden in 1987. The inscription reads: "Isacco Sacerdoti restored the former Cappello palace, now Malipiero." The garden dates back to this period: the area is divided by two intersecting avenues, each lined with flower beds bordered by low boxwood hedges. The Gothic wellhead is the central vanishing point of a composition flanked by the Grand Canal on one side and the "Temple of Neptune," a sculp-

F. Bagnara, sketch for the setting of the first act of Oreste at La Fenice theater, 1834–35 season. Collection Correr Museum. Photograph courtesy of the Correr Museum.

tural group, on the other. The perspective thus created gives the impression of a much larger space, evoking once more the secret "delights" of a former Veneto-Byzantine palace.

After the Congress of Vienna in 1815, the Austrians regained Venice, but the properties of the dispossessed religious orders were not returned. Many became gardens.

In 1834, Count Spiridione Papadópoli en-

71. Ibid.

72. Ibid. See also Venice: A. Rubin de Cervin Albrizzi Archive, Reg. 47 e B. 177, containing Meduna's 1862 appraisal.

73. G. Damerini, La Ca' Grande dei Cappello e dei Malipiero (Castelfranco, Veneto: Grifone-Grafiche Trevisan, 1962), pp. 93, 184, 197, 202.

gaged the architect Francesco Bagnara on an important project. Bagnara, born in Vicenza in 1784, had attended the Academy of Fine Arts in Venice thanks to the patronage of Count Germanico Angaràn, who entrusted him to the tutelage of the landscape painter Borsato. In 1838, this latter obtained full professorship and the chair of landscape painting at the Academy. He dedicated himself to stage design as well.

Count Papadópoli purchased and had surveyed the entire estate of the ex-convent of the Cross at the Tolentini. He demolished the buildings and annexed some adjacent gardens, entrusting the resulting expanse of land to Bagnara to create a garden.[74]

The painter took advantage of the old convent wall, inserting in it a neo-Gothic turret on the canal side to create a belvedere, a recurring and essential feature of gardens of the period.

The choice of English-style landscaping was dictated not only by the fashion of the time but by Bagnara's personal taste for the picturesque, imitating "the unruliness of nature, tempered by the expedient of comfort . . . with rustic buildings and ruins, artificial lakes, bridges, cloister-topped hillocks, and

G. Pividor and J. Barozzi, Entrance to the Papadópoli Gardens, engraving, nineteenth century. Collection Correr Museum. Photograph courtesy of the Correr Museum.

grassy dales."[75] The project even included a grove for free-roaming gazelles, and pheasants from Mexico and China. The water for the waterfalls was collected and channelled into the small lake, and there were hothouses for citrus, mostly orange trees. Rare species of camellias, dahlias and *araucaria excelsa* were grown under the direction of the head gardener, Tommaso Fedeli.[76]

The Papadópoli garden was an important example of English-style landscaping, highly praised by Pietro Selvatico, who favorably compared its "picturesque variety of pleasant aspects" to the coldness of Selva's Napoleonic Gardens. The great charm of this garden did not withstand changes in fashion. In 1863, a French architect, Marc Guignon, relandscaped it in an altogether different manner.[77]

Another nineteenth-century garden lies behind the Patriarchal Seminary next to the Salute Church. The seminary was originally in Murano, but in 1817 was moved to the house of the Somaschi Fathers, one of the religious institutions dissolved with the Napoleonic edicts.[78] The present-day garden covers an area once largely belonging to the gardens of Cà Pozzo, which were linked to the building housing the Fathers. The garden is not well known, but Moschini records that it was designed by Alberto Parolini at the time of the transfer of the seminary.[79]

The garden owned by Luigi Borghi and Virginia Tabaglio, located in the parish of Ognisanti, was created in the latter half of the nineteenth century. Although it did not boast any particular architectural feature, it contained an enormous variety of flowers. Cecchetto mentions the prizes awarded to the roses and the trailing plants in the 1871 flower show organized by the Lombard Horticultural Society, and the awards from the Veneto Institute of Letters, Science, and Art (1871–72) for the grafting techniques em-

74. G. Damerini, Scenografi veneziani dell'Ottocento (Venice: Pozza, 1962), pp. 9, 102.

75. N. Ivanoff, "Uno scenografo romantico veneziano Francesco Bagnara (1784–1866)," Ateneo Veneto, 127, nos. 3–4, Mar.-Apr. 1940): 101.

76. F. Gera, Principali giardini di Venezia, p. 14. See also B. Cecchetti, Una passeggiata nel giardino Papadopoli (Venice: Visentini, 1887); P. Bussadori, Il giardino e la scena (Castelfranco, Veneto: MP, 1986), p. 97.

77. G. Damerini, Scenografi veneziani, p. 9; M. Tlurvurd, Amsterdam et Venise (Paris: n.p., 1876); La Gazzetta di Venezia, 3, 1921: 14.

78. G.A. Moschini, Chiesa e Seminario di S. M. della Salute (Venice: Antonelli, 1842), p. 108.

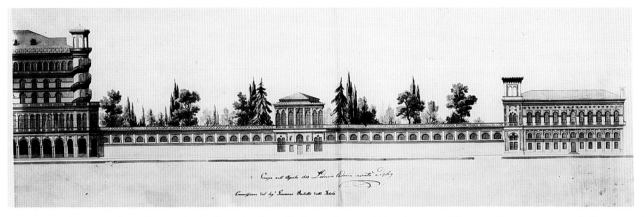

L. Cadorin, Garden of a palace to be built on the Riva degli Schiavoni, ink and watercolor, 1853. Collection Correr Museum. Photograph courtesy of the Correr Museum.

ployed there. The garden was rather small, only 6.5 square meters, but its rose bushes were so numerous that in May the effect was overwhelming.[80]

The so-called "Garden of Eden" enjoys greater renown. Its proprietor, F. Eden (his actual name was Hyden), was an Englishman who came to the Giudecca late in the nineteenth century to cure his consumption. On the site of a former fruit and vegetable garden, he created a prototypical garden in the English style, replete with ancient artifacts. The garden remained intact through a succession of owners, only to fall prey to the flood that ravaged the city in 1966. At the time, the garden was the property of Princess Aspasia of Greece. In 1977, it was rented for a time to the American art historian Elizabeth Gardner, who "with the spirit of a New England pioneer, brought the garden back to its former vigor, replanting the rose bushes and the magnolia grove, and restoring the "Moorish" kiosk set in the very heart of the luxuriant vegetation."[81]

Today the new owner, another Englishman, is letting nature take the upper hand. His intent is to create a corner free from the self-conscious "naturalism" that characterized English landscaping of the Romantic age. Conceptually, the garden today is much closer to a Japanese model, attuned to the values of simplicity and natural beauty.

A small empty lot next to Sansovino's Palazzo Corner on the Grand Canal once housed Antonio Canova's first studio. There, the artist shaped "Dedalus and Icarus," the statue commissioned by Procurator Pietro Vettor Pisani and originally placed at the water-side entrance of his palace at San Polo. Today the statue is in the Correr Museum.[82]

In 1896, Prince Frederich Hohenlohe had a small house built on the site, and called it *Casetta Rossa*, "the little red house," or *casetta delle rose*, "the house of the roses," because of the roses planted in its small garden overlooking the Grand Canal. Prince Frederick was from the Austrian branch of the Hohenlohe dynasty, but had been born in Venice and spoke even Venetian dialect fluently. He was a diplomat and the brother of Maria Thurn und Taxis, the patroness of poet Rainer Maria Rilke. The prince interrupted his diplomatic career to settle in Venice, where he commissioned the architect Rupolo to build the "little red house" for him. He lived there until the outbreak of the First World War.

In October 1915, the house was rented, through the offices of painter Mariano Fortuny, to Gabriele d'Annunzio, who remained there with his daughter Renata until 1918. The poet, temporarily blind and recovering from wounds received when a plane he was piloting was forced down at sea, wrote his *Notturno* in the little house. To mark his residence, he planted a pomegranate tree in the garden. The tree still stands on the manicured lawn, a lasting memento of a significant presence.

In 1959 and 1963, the architect Carlo Scarpa restored the ground floor of the Palazzo Querini-Stampalia at Santa Maria Formosa. The palace today serves as the seat of a foundation established and funded by the late Giovanni Querini-Stampalia, the last descendant of a noble Venetian family.[83] The garden, also renovated, dates to around 1528; it is attributed to Guglielmo de' Grigi, often called "Il

79. Guida del Seminario patriarcale *(Venice: Tipografia San Marco, 1912), p. 110.*

80. B. Cecchetti, *Del giardino dei Signori Luigi Borghi e Virginia Tabaglio in Venezia (Venice: P. Varatovich, 1888).*

81. N. Pozza, "Giardini inventati dall'allegrezza," Ville e giardini, monumenti d'Italia *(Novara: Istituto Geografico De Agostini, 1984), p. 138. See also F. Eden, A Garden in Venice (London: published at the Office of Country Life by G. Newnes, 1903).*

82. I. Chiappini di Sorio, *Palazzo Pisani Moretta, p. 39.*

Bergamasco."[84] The palace rises on the site of a smaller residence, clearly visible on the de' Barbari map. The newer building is hemmed in by the same streets and canals as the building it replaced, and for that reason it is unlikely that it occupies a larger site than its predecessor.

The present-day garden reflects the dimensions of the fifteenth-century original, and is dwarfed by the sixteenth-century palace that adjoins it. The

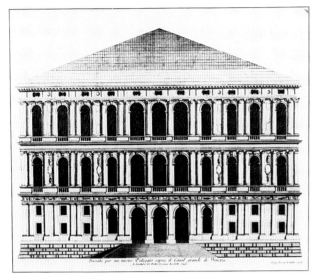

G. Fossati, Palazzo Venier dei Leoni on the Grand Canal, engraving, 1749. Collection Correr Museum. Photograph courtesy of the Correr Museum.

level of the garden is higher than that of the ground floor of the house, in deference to the habitual arrangement of the period. The landscaping is decidedly modern, however, with Japanese overtones. Scarpa's plans respect the particular values of the restricted space; the vegetation harmoniously blends into the larger framework of the building, striking a balance between lawn and fountain. This latter is flattened almost flush with the ground, a still pool whose water lilies provide the only note of color in an otherwise entirely green setting.

Another landscape restoration has been carried out at Palazzo Venier dei Leoni, which today houses the Peggy Guggenheim Collection. Only the ground floor and the flight of steps on the Grand

Canal were built according to the original plans by Lorenzo Boschetti in 1749.[85] The small interior garden, many times restored, has been painstakingly redesigned by architect Giorgio Bellavitis.

The history and reversals of fortune of the gardens of Venice have infrequently been charted by modern historians, who are generally more attentive to developments on the mainland. But if comparison with the more celebrated gardens of central Italy does not always favor Venetian examples, these latter are laudable nonetheless because of their fidelity to the unique characteristics of the Venetian environment: its limited space and uninspiring flat terrain.

Neglect is responsible for the wild state of many of these gardens. There are a few excellent exceptions, mostly recently restored. If these latter gardens lack a "history" or a precise scheme, they are nevertheless important signs of a renewed compassion for nature.

The visitor approaching Venice today by air will glimpse a closely knit urban plan studded with green jewels. The same visitor may be frustrated if he tries to discover many of the gardens that had beckoned so promisingly, as many no longer exist or are in private hands. However, a nineteenth-century itinerary is easily followed, as the public gardens are there for all to see.

Rooftop terraces have supplanted the formal garden for many Venetians. Plants, some extremely large, are potted along the edges of terraces, alternating with statuary to create an impromptu garden. Glimpsed from the street or the boardwalk along a canal, these snatches of greenery suggest the fascination of the secret gardens of another era, evoking the "intellectual delights" once woven into the incredible urban fabric of Venice.

D. Gasparoni, The garden of the "bombarde" in the Arsenal of Venice, engraving, 1779. Collection Correr Museum. Photograph courtesy of the Correr Museum.

83. G. Mazzariol, "Un'opera di Carlo Scarpa: il giardino di un antico palazzo veneziano," Zodiac, no. 13, 1964: 40.

84. E. Merkel, Catalogo della pinacoteca della Fondazione Querini Stampalia (Venice; Pozza. 1979), p. 16.

85. Venice: Correr Museum, Prints P.D.2336–2337. See also S. Biadene, Le Venezie possibili (Milan: Electa, 1985), p. 134.

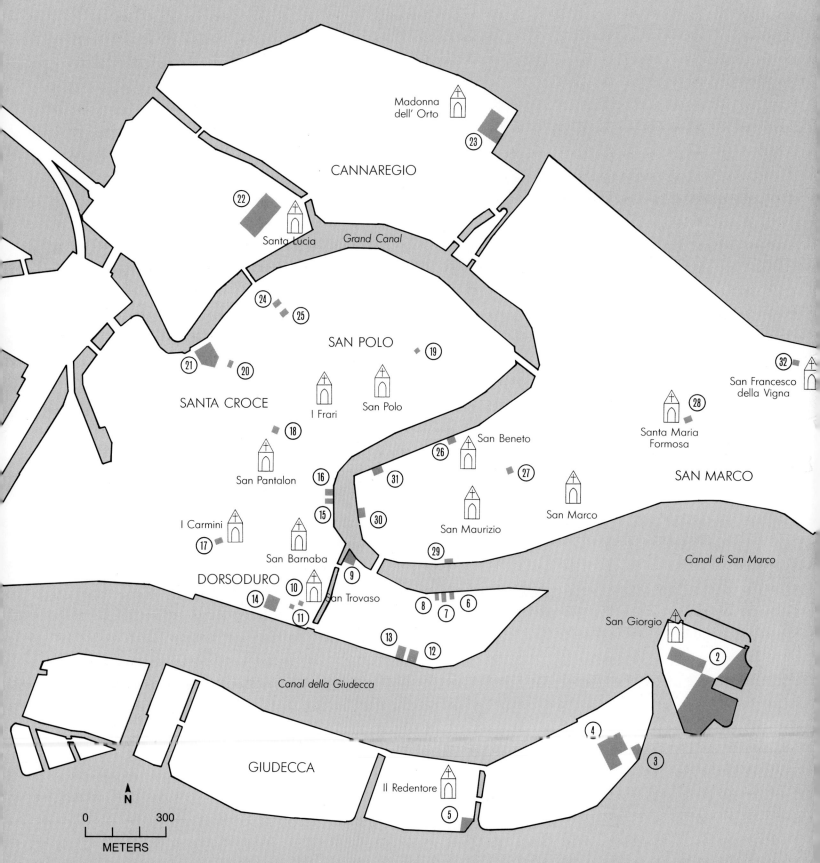

THE GARDENS OF VENICE

Madonna
dell' Orto

㉓

CANNAREGIO

㉒

Santa Lucia   *Grand Canal*

㉔   ㉕

SAN POLO   ⑲   ㉜

San Francesco
della Vigna

㉑   ⑳

SANTA CROCE

I Frari   San Polo

㉘

Santa Maria
Formosa

⑱   San Beneto

San Pantalon   ⑯   ㉖

㉛   SAN MARCO

I Carmini   ⑮   ㉚

San Maurizio   San Marco

⑰   San Barnaba

㉙

DORSODURO   ⑩   *Canal di San Marco*

⑭   San Trovaso

⑪   ⑧ ⑦ ⑥

⑨

San Giorgio

⑬

⑫   ②

Canal della Giudecca

④

③

GIUDECCA

Il Redentore

⑤

0   300

METERS

N

MURANO

San Donato

0   300
METERS

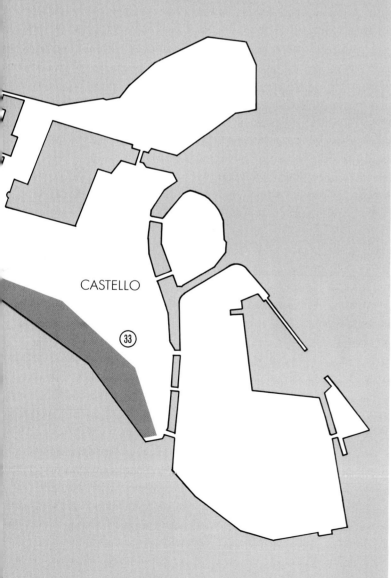

CASTELLO

(33)

The locations of the gardens included in this book are shown on the map presented here. While many of the gardens are in private hands, some are open to the public or can be glimpsed from the numerous canals, bridges, or walkways of Venice. This information is provided below to enable curious visitors to see the city's gardens for themselves. The best months for the gardens are: May, June, September, and October.

1. Palazzo Giustiniani, now the Murano Glass Museum. Courtyard open to the public.
2. San Giorgio Maggiore gardens, cloisters, and the "Green Theater." Permission to visit may be obtained from the Giorgio Cini Foundation.
3. Hotel Cipriani gardens. Open to guests of the hotel. For non-guests, permission to visit may be obtained from the Hotel Cipriani.
4. The Vineyards of Casanova. Permission to visit may be obtained from the Hotel Cipriani.
5. Ca'Leone gardens. Private. They can be seen from a boat on the lagoon.
6. Palazzo Dario garden. Private. It may be seen from the Campiello Barbaro or from the San Cristoforo bridge.
7. Palazzo Venier dei Leoni, now the Peggy Guggenheim Foundation. Garden open to the public.
8. Palazzo da Mula Morosini terraces and altane. Private.
9. Palazzo Contarini Corfù dagli Scrigni Rocca courtyard and garden. Private.
10, 11. San Trovaso gardens. Private.
12. Connie and Natale Rusconi garden. Private.
13. Rocca garden. Private. It may be seen from the Fondamenta degli Incurabili or the Ponte Lungo at the Zattere.
14. Palazzo Guistiniani Recanati courtyard and garden. Private. They can be seen from the Fondamenta Bonlini or the Trevisan bridge.
15. Palazzo Nani Lucheschi garden. Private.
16. Palazzo Giustiniani Brandolini garden. Private.
17. Palazzo Zenobio garden. Permission to visit may be obtained from the Armenian College.
18. Palazzo Dolfin courtyard and garden. Permission to visit may be obtained from the University of Venice.
19. Palazzo Albrizzi garden. Private. It may be seen from the Ponte delle Tette or from a boat on the Rio San Cassiano.
20. Institute of Architecture courtyard. Open to the public.
21. Papadópoli Gardens. Open to the public.
22. Palazzo Savorgnan garden. Open to the public.
23. Palazzo Contarini dal Zaffo gardens. Private. They can be seen by boat or from the Fondamente Nuove.
24. Palazzo Gradenigo at Rio Marin garden. Private. It may be seen from the Rio Marin.
25. Palazzo Soranzo Cappello at Rio Marin garden. Private.
26. Palazzo Volpi di Misurata courtyard. Private.
27. Palazzo Contarini dal Bovolo courtyard. Open to the public.
28. Palazzo Querini Stampalia garden. Permission to visit may be obtained from the Querini-Stampalia Foundation.
29. Casetta Rossa garden. Private. It may be seen from a boat on the Grand Canal.
30. Palazzo Malpiero Capello garden. Private. It may be seen from a boat on the Grand Canal.
31. Palazzi Mocenigo at San Samuele garden. Private.
32. San Francesco della Vigna garden and cloisters. Permission to visit may be obtained from the church officers.
33. The Napoleonic Gardens. Open to the public.

Left: *The first cloister of the monastery of San Giorgio Maggiore.*

Overleaf: *San Giorgio Maggiore, drawn in 1743.*

3 Islands in the Lagoon

Once it was the gardens of the outlying islands that filled the market baskets of Venice. Fruit and vegetable harvests from the churches and their surrounding properties were bountiful. The gardens were often quite ornamental, with Byzantine, Gothic, and Renaissance influences. Monastery food gardens included flowers and evergreen trees laid out with style and grace.

The island of San Giorgio, once called the Island of Cypresses, and green with monastery vegetable gardens, vineyards, and orchards, was a sanctuary for popes and doges, and was enriched by their bounty. After a century of neglect, it is again a place of peace.

The second cloister of this Benedictine center, planned by architect Giovanni di Antonio Buora, was built by his son Andrea. Tall cypresses stand serene in panels of Bermuda grass.

Who layeth the beams of his chambers
in the waters: who maketh the clouds
his chariot: who walketh upon the
wings of the wind:

PSALM 104:3

The church of San Giorgio Maggiore, Andrea Palladio's vision of a classically beautiful church, lifts the spirits and the sights to greater things. Under the pink and blue skies of Tiepolo, the burning sunsets of Turner, the church, seen for the first time, makes one gasp with joy at such an expression of God and man.

The spectacular natural placement of the island of San Giorgio Maggiore, opposite the Piazzetta of San Marco, is why it is called the jewel of the Venetian lagoon. It was because of its nearness to the Doge's Palace that Doge Tribuno Memmo in 982 gave the island to Giovanni Morosini to establish a Benedictine monastery. For centuries the church and monastery were a retreat for prelates and patricians, and prospered from their beneficence. Venice's most skilled architects contributed to the splendor of the buildings, and her finest artists and scholars to their treasures.

Napoleon's arrival, and the fall of the Republic, saw the precious contents of the center looted, and its mission of enlightenment suppressed. This interruption of a brilliant history lasted until the middle of this century when, in 1951, the State accepted the proposal of Count Vittorio Cini to restore the church and monastery to their former glory in memory of his son Count Giorgio Cini.

The Giorgio Cini Foundation is responsible for the magnificent restoration of the church, the monastery, the gardens, the construction of an open-air amphitheatre, and the creation of two schools and three institutes. The island is once again a place for the study of culture and civilization. The world is drawn to its shores. As the site of two recent world summit meetings, it continues to fulfill its destiny.

And he shewed me a pure river of water
of life, clear as crystal, proceeding
out of the throne of God and of the Lamb.
    In the midst of the street of it,
and on either side of the river, *was*
there the tree of life, which bare
twelve *manner* of fruits, *and* yielded
her fruit every month: and the leaves
of the tree *were* for the healing of
the nations.

REVELATION 22:1–2

The first cloister, the work of Andrea Palladio, with seventeenth-century alterations by Baldassarre Longhena, was once filled with cypresses. The garden's present design is based on an elaborate pattern found in an eighteenth-century engraving.

Overleaf: *Tree-lined walks lead to the "Green Theater," outlined with cypress. Rising rows of marble seats are bordered with dwarf Japanese holly hybrid. An elevator ride to the top of the campanile offers a sweeping view of Venice, and the natural beauty of the island.*

54

Ca'Leone is a house that speaks for a Giudecca of the sixteenth century, when noble families had roomy villas there, with spacious gardens that spilled into the lagoon. The island was famous for its vineyards and open fields where Venetians enjoyed holiday picnics nearer to the cooling breezes of the sea.

Ca' Leone retains its history and charm. A front path to the water's edge is shaded by oleander, cypress, and southern magnolia. Rose trees, salvia, zinnias, and nicotiana are among the flowers that line the walk. The view is toward the lagoon.

Ca' Leone was part of the Guidecca holdings of the powerful Cornaro family, bankers with palaces from Dalmatia to Cyprus and monopolies in the salt, mining, shipping, and slave trades.

The young and beautiful Caterina Cornaro, Queen of Cyprus, was covered with jewels and given a palace in Venice and a castle in Asolo when the Venetian Republic took over her island kingdom. In addition to Cyprus, the Cornaro family gave Venice four doges and a number of procurators, generals, and cardinals.

In 1549, Pietro Aretino wrote to Benedetto Cornaro: "If Guidecca did not merit admiration for the beauty of its palaces and churches, the garden greening around your *nobile* rooms would show the people how marvelous the island is."

Several houses of the Cornaro remain: Ca'Leone and Casa Frollo, which now belong to the Count Volpi di Misurata, and a house and garden still referred to as "the garden of Eden." At the turn of this century, Englishman F. Eden rescued one of Giudecca's largest gardens, and described giving it new life in a delightful book entitled *A Garden in Venice*. Charming illustrations show pergolas of flowering vines, roses and lillies in profusion, winding paths, shady arbors, sparkling fountains, and lemon trees in giant terra-cotta pots bordering a reflecting pool. Eden wrote:

As much as possible we give Nature her head . . .

The result is that from early spring to late autumn we see a mass of bloom. The daphne tells us spring has come, and we are snow white with Marinelli, the only cherry which will stand our salt air and soil. Then pink with peach blossom, sweet with lilac, gay with may, Forsythia, Deutsia, Spirea, Weigelea, and Azalea. . . .

The Eden garden had an abundance of mulberry, the succulent, purply fruit Venetians eat on the Feast of the Redentore when they watch the fireworks from their boats that fill the lagoon with twinkling lights till dawn. Eden wrote: "Among our young women visitors are some who are fond of mulberries, and we advise the prettiest ones to pick with their lips."

In Eden's day the monks from the Redentore monastery sought flower and fruit branches from his garden. They "made large garlands of Mantegna type for the decoration of the church and doorway," a celebration of nature in this splendid work of Andrea Palladio.

Herringbone brick paths lead from the house to the lagoon, a decorative iron gate, and a landing for visiting boats. An old cypress bends with the breeze. A border of Coreopsis "moonglow" is lush with color. The rose of Sharon is a reminder that Chinese hibiscus was introduced to Venice via the exotic trade routes through Syria.

Overleaf: *The annuals flourishing in these bright beds and borders include zinnias, snapdragons, salvia, sweet alyssum, and ageratum. Trees include juniper, magnolia, and cypress. Vines frame the dovecote and cling tenaciously to the chimneys.*

G iudecca, for centuries an island of gardens, was once a haven for Michelangelo and a haunt for Casanova. The vineyards around Palladio's church, Il Redentore, and the flower gardens of the Hotel Cipriani are reminders that Giudecca is still one of the greenest islands in the lagoon.

A panoramic view of the Casanova vineyards, with the domes of the churches of Le Zitelle and Santa Maria della Salute in the distance.

Overleaf: *Luxurious expanses of green make the gardens of the Hotel Cipriani seem far from the Gothic madness of* the Grand Canal. In his book Daily Life in Venice in the Time of Casanova, Maurice Andrieux wrote:

The first meeting, for chocolate, took place late in the morning, for early rising was no part of the routine. This moment, wrote Goldini's Jesuit acquaintance, the versifier Giambattista Roberti, with its 'spicy sips and spicier conversation,' was 'the most delightful that friendship could contrive or afford.' The stimulating chatter continued in long walks round the gardens, ideal settings for elegant flirtation under the indulgent gaze of marble nymph and satyr.

G ardens and glass have inspired each other on the island of Murano since the thirteenth century. In the ancient Palazzo Giustiniani, now the Murano Glass Museum, there are some four thousand examples of this spectacular Venetian art.

Green vines dramatize the architecture of the Murano Glass Museum courtyard, which includes a random planting of Virginia creeper, English ivy, aucuba, mulberry, oleander, and loquat.

A most intriguing mix of architecture, Palazzo Giustiniani in Murano, now the Murano Glass Museum, is the ancient seat of the Bishops of Torcello. It was built for Bishop Marco Giustiniani in 1669, over a fifteenth-century Gothic building of which an arcade and a few other elements remain.

Even though the glass factories were in full production during the sixteenth century, Murano was a favorite gathering place for artists and humanists who wanted to retreat from the city.

Julia M. Ady wrote of the gardens in Murano in an article titled "Venetian Scholars and Their Gardens," in the October 1914 issue of *The Nineteenth Century*:

. . . it is difficult to realise that this island was once famous for its sumptuous pleasure-houses and gardens. Yet so it was in the days of Gaspare Contarini and Pietro Bembo, of Titian and Aretino. Then poets and travelers alike extolled Murano as the most delightful place in the world, dear above all to scholars and thinkers, and meet to be the home of nymphs and goddesses. They praise its balmy breezes and sparkling fountains, its fields of musk and damask roses, of violets and narcissus, its groves of citron and orange, and beds of sweet-smelling mint, of rosemary and lavender.

The Flemish scholar Christophe Longueil, described a visit to Murano in a letter to Bembo in June 1520:

I have been at Venice for a fortnight and spent a week of the greatest enjoyment with our dear friend, Messer Andrea Navagero, in his country house at Murano. The garden belonging to this villa was a very pleasant sight, since all the trees in the orchard and plantations are laid out in the form of a quincunx. All the trees and hedges are clipped in different shapes, and are exquisite examples of topiary art. The sight, indeed, greatly exceeded my highest expectations. The apple trees are all planted in regular rows, at discreet intervals, and have grown with amazing rapidity, since they were put in the ground by our Navagero himself, only a few months ago. Nothing could be more beautiful in shape and colour, nothing sweeter in smell and taste, or more excellent in size and variety, than the fruit which this orchard bears.

Gardens and glass have flourished side by side on Murano since the late thirteenth century, when the glassworks were moved to the island to help guard the Venetian secret of glassmaking. Recognized and collected all over the world, Venetian glass is prized for its luminous color, ethereal texture and transparency, and often for its fantasy flower forms inspired by the gardens of Murano.

In 1861, the Giustiniani palace became the Murano Glass Museum under the direction of Abbot Vincenzo Zanetti. The courtyard is still a haven for rambling green vines and plants typical of the area. Carved wellheads add the drama of sculpture.

Overleaf: The architecture of several centuries is evident in this Murano palace, from the fifteenth-century arcade to the seventeenth-century façade of Istrian stone, and the eighteenth-century iron grillwork. Stone figures stand in niches on either side of the gate that opens to a view of vineyard and orchard beyond. An ornamental loquat tree reminds one that the sun is kind to this island in the Venetian lagoon.

San Francesco della
Vigna cloister.

Overleaf: *Typical
Renaissance church
garden.*

Second overleaf:
*Church of San
Francesco della Vigna,
named for the vineyard
given to the friars in
1253.*

Up to the 17th Century

An appreciation of nature's gifts was essential to Renaissance enlightenment. As never before, gardens enhanced the beauty and quality of life. Sansovino and Palladio were designing buildings in harmony with their surroundings, while the Bellinis, Carpaccio, Titian, Tintoretto, and Veronese were celebrating life in their art. The enthusiasm for nature was taken up in Venice, bringing fresh energy to gardening.

S urrounding the church of San Trovaso are properties once occupied by clergy and craftsmen. Several of the small houses are now lived in by artists. Their gardens add much charm to the quarter.

The pergola at the house of artist Liselotte Höhs-Manera is a dense weaving of many vines including English ivy and Virginia creeper. The figure, from a group of the four seasons, depicts Winter, and is typical of the work of the Bonazza family, eighteenth-century Venetian stonecutters.

San Trovaso is typical of many churches in Venice that developed as centers of living surrounded by the houses and gardens of patricians, and were enriched by art commissioned by them. The church existed in the tenth century, was rebuilt in 1068, and again in 1584. The church gives onto a *campo*, or square, and a *rio*, or narrow canal, of the same name. The Campo San Trovaso is interesting for its planting of tall, lacy-top trees, and its raised platform covering clay cases used for purifying rainwater collected in the wells—a good place to sit and study the campanile, or the passing parade. The Rio San Trovaso is a quick route from the Giudecca Canal to the Grand Canal, and on its bank is the colorful squero, or boat yard, of the gondola builders that has inspired artists for centuries.

During the Renaissance, churches and convents were numerous in Venice, and many of their gardens were splendid. In 1494, a Milanese canon wrote in his journal: "I cannot refrain from repeating that nothing has surprised me more in this city than the many beautiful gardens which are to be seen here, especially, I must say, those belonging to the different religious orders." In *Coryat's Crudities*, published in 1611, the English traveler Thomas Coryat included this description:

... as I have before said; their streets, their churches, their monasteries, their market places, and all their other public building of rare magnificence; also many fair gardens replenished with diversity of delicate fruits, as oranges, citrons, lemons, apricots, musk melons, angurias, and what not. . . .

Around the church of San Trovaso, palaces and small houses with gardens continue to flourish with flowers and fruits that are a part of Venice's history.

One of the gardens of San Trovaso is a hidden enclosure rich with green. The plantings are many and varied, including Virginia creeper, wisteria, hydrangea, and rosemary. Prospering under the watchful eye of its owner, the garden offers visitors a refreshing green experience.

P

alazzo Giustiniani Recanati, like several houses along the Zattere, has a fine garden that prospers from the warm moist air from the Giudecca Canal, and the numerous hazy summer days that bless Venice.

A horse chestnut helps to shield the Giustiniani Recanati garden courtyard from the brightest sun. Spring bulbs and English ivy border the pool, and pots of camellias add color throughout Venice's extended summer season.

The garden entrance of Palazzo Giustiniani Recanati is surrounded by a wall of Virginia creeper, or American vine, as Venetians call this summer-green-to-autumn-red wall covering that is rampant and so rewarding in the gardens of Venice. The horse chestnut, in autumn color, and the wisteria that climbs the pergola give welcome shade.

Overleaf: *The rooftop garden is a pleasant place to gather on summer evenings, and offers a refreshing vista from the indoor sitting room where visitors are often received on summer afternoons. Virginia creeper enfolds a figure of the Madonna, shielded from the sun by a canopy, a Venetian tradition.*

In the sixteenth century, in the parish of San Trovaso, the botanist and scholar Pier Antonio Michiel planted an unusual and splendid garden, with rare herbals for medicinal use. This is the same Michiel who founded the famous and influential Botanical Garden in Padua. Next to this site, just on the other side of the Trevisan Bridge, is the Palazzo Giustiniani Recanati, an impressive building that runs through to the Zattere. The Giustiniani family provided Venice with great leadership, and more, a saint—Saint Lorenzo Giustiniani. A number of Giustiniani palaces are scattered throughout Venice; this particular one has been a repository of great collections of art, porcelain, and books, and is still very much a protected family enclave. The courtyard and rooftop gardens have a quality unique to Venice, which George Sand described so well in a letter dated May 1834 and published in *Lettres d'un Voyageur:*

. . . the flowers of Venice, brought to light in this warm clayey soil, blossoming in this damp atmosphere, have a freshness, a richness of tissue, and a languor of attitude which makes them resemble the women of this climate, whose beauty is as brilliant and evanescent as their own. The double flowering bramble climbs round every pillar, and suspends its garlands of white rosettes from the black arabesques of the balconies. The vanilla iris, the Persian tulip, so beautifully striped with pure red and white that it seems formed from the material in which the ancient Venetians used to dress, Greek roses, and pyramids of gigantic campanulas are heaped in the vases which cover the balustrades. Sometimes there is quite an arbor of honeysuckle crowning the balcony from one end to the other . . . At every street corner, the Madonna shelters her mysterious lamp under a jasmine canopy . . .

In 1487, when Giovanni Dario embellished this simple Gothic house with a much-ornamented façade on the Grand Canal side, he dedicated it to "the spirit of the city," and had the dedication chiseled in the stone foundation. The present owners do not mind the fascination of passersby and encourage their pocket garden to give a bonus of growing green, flowers, and fragrance.

Palazzo Dario, small and delicious like a tiny decorated wedding cake, is an appealing example of two styles of Venetian architecture—Gothic and Renaissance Lombardesque. The garden, with flourishing vines and flowering shrubs tumbling over the walls, can be admired from the San Cristoforo Bridge.

Oleander, wisteria
rhododendron, and
azalea—offering the
visitor the same rewards
found in a large garden
in the country—are part
of the informal scheme
of this tiny, walled
garden at Palazzo Dario
in Venice. In the essay
"The Grand Canal" in
Italian Hours, Henry
James wrote of this
house:

. . . the delightful little
Palazzo Dario, intimately
familiar to English and
American travellers,
picks itself out in the
foreshortened
brightness. The Dario is
covered with the
loveliest little marble
plates and sculptured
circles; it is made up of
exquisite pieces—as if
there had been only
enough to make it
small—so that it looks, in
its extreme antiquity, a
good deal like a house
of cards that hold
together by a tenure it
would be fatal to touch.

Palazzo Dario has
enchanted writers for
centuries. A marker on
the Campiello Barbaro
side commemorates
visits to the house by the
French writer Henri de
Règnier, and his works
inspired by the city.

Palazzo Contarini dal Bovolo, with its famous spiral staircase and five floors of arched loggias, is a fantasy, almost a folly, and a gem example of late-fifteenth-century architecture in the Gothic style. Vines, shrubs, and artifacts decorate the entrance courtyard.

The architectural delights of Palazzo Contarini dal Bovolo sparkle in full sun. The green includes pitosporum and English ivy.

One of the more than twenty-five Contarini palaces in Venice, Palazzo Contarini dal Bovolo is certainly the most startling and amusing on the Calle della Vida side. This is the palace of the famous spiral staircase (*bovolo* is a snail shell in Venetian dialect). Built circa 1499 in the late Gothic style, it is thought to be the work of Giovanni Candi, and considered an interesting example of Lombardesque construction.

The Contarinis, who gave Venice eight doges, often named their palaces after some aspect of the buildings themselves—Contarini dagli Scrigni (of the money chests), Contarini della Porta di Ferro (of the iron door), Contarini delle Figure (of the figures). This last one is said to have been haunted since the fifteenth century by a beautiful heiress who, together with her fortune and her palace, was gambled away by a rogue husband.

Palazzo Contarini dal Bovolo always delights. Travel writer Hugh Honor suggested that "it is well worth seeing when the the light of the full moon glitters on its marble arcade." The small enclosure in front, with its scattering of vines and shrubs, can hardly be called a garden, but it has become a resting place for several fine old wellheads and other architectural fragments. Venice's cats find these stones a perfect place to take the sun.

The entrance to the spiral staircase at Palazzo Contarini dal Bovolo seen through a weaving of English ivy. An iron fence encloses the courtyard filled with several finely carved old wellheads and other examples of the art of Venetian stonecutters.

A spacious garden at Palazzo Contarini Corfù dagli Scrigni Rocca is a particular surprise because of its varied plantings, objects, and influences. Ornamental and subtropical fruit trees— loquat, orange, and plum — contribute fragrance, decorative fruit, and a feeling of the exotic.

Eight doges brought the large Contarini family much fame and fortune. Vigorous in battles to expand the Republic and active in the rule at home, the Contarinis are responsible for numerous palaces, among them, two that stand together on the Grand Canal near the Accademia Bridge: the fifteenth-century Gothic Palazzo Contarini Corfù and the Palazzo Contarini dagli Scrigni, built in 1609, the work of Palladio's disciple Vincenzo Scamozzi. The concept of joining two palaces follows the Venetian custom of building an adjacent palace to enlarge the entertaining rooms of a palace not able to contain a family growing in power and prestige.

In 1524, a niece of Doge Andrea Gritti married Paolo Contarini. The festivities were so splendid that they are still talked about. After a glittering ceremony in the church of San Marco and a lavish dinner, the large wedding party of aristocrats bordered the Bucintoro, the ducal barge normally used only once each year to sail to the Adriatic, where the marriage of Venice to the sea is celebrated by throwing a golden ring into the sea. This time, the Bucintoro sailed up the Grand Canal to the Rio San Trovaso, where the Contarini palace was decorated with colorful tapestries, ablaze with lights, and filled with music. There was dancing till dawn. The last Contarini to live in these palaces was Alvise II, who gave his impressive collection of nearly two hundred paintings to found the Galleria dell'Accademia.

The present owner, Count Giulio Rocca, born in the palace, takes great pleasure in its unique character and place in Venetian history. Today the classic Gothic detailing is enriched with eccentricities accumulated through the ages. The pungent colors of various plasters, a wide assortment of marble and stone figures, stained-glass windows of brilliant color next to faded murals on the courtyard façade, and a staircase that goes nowhere give the house and garden a sense of mystery, and a certain magic.

Three of the four young god figures which stand on the wall separating the Contarini courtyard from the garden. Flowering shrubs and trees offer shade and color, and a stage for an interesting collection of stone carvings and figures.

At the Contarini palace there is a great mix of color in the plantings—including loquat, oleander and orange trees. Stained glass in the entrance windows adds brilliance, and contrast with the faded murals high on the courtyard façade.

Overleaf: An ancient loquat tree shades the staircase that goes nowhere. The prolific vines include Virginia creeper, grape, and English ivy. A stone head, probably a young god, stands with boxes of friendly, old-fashioned impatiens.

The Madonna dell'Orto church campanile overlooking the garden of the Palazzo Contarini dal Zaffo.

Overleaf: Contarini garden, drawn by Guardi.

Second overleaf: Garden and Casino degli Spiriti, seen from the Lagoon.

17th Century

In this age of Baroque design, and the architecture of Scamozzi and Longhena, the marriage of landscape and architecture was taking place in the countryside on a sweeping scale. In Venice, green, growing things gained significance as coverings or added decoration for architecture, and were cultivated with enthusiasm in courtyards and walled enclosures.

Mocenigo—palaces of poetry and power; home to a family of Doges and to Lord Byron while he lived in the city of his dreams and passions. The courtyard, staged like a theatrical backdrop, was conceived in the days of Palladio.

Just inside the Mocenigo gate: the family coat of arms is dominated by two roses, in the Gothic style. A covered walkway Is shaded by Virginia creeper and a palmetto. The garden statue, patrician and refined in detail, may symbolize Spring.

The Mocenigo family gave Venice seven doges and four grand palaces. On the Grand Canal, near San Samuele, the palaces stand in a row: the Palazzo Mocenigo Vecchio, the oldest; the double Mocenigo palace reconstructed in the eighteenth century to enlarge the sixteenth-century Palazzo Mocenigo Nero, the one nearest the Rialto Bridge. The buildings are referred to now simply as Casa Vecchia and Casa Nuova.

Palazzo Mocenigo Nero was commissioned by Alvise Mocenigo I. Construction began in 1570, the year he was elected Doge. Two engravings from the early eighteenth century and a recent study indicate that the palazzo included work of Andrea Palladio. Although there are things Palladian in the building's character, the idea is much debated. Palladio was linked to the Mocenigo family by several major commissions he received from Mocenigo doges, including Il Redentore and the great arch and loggia on the Grand Canal that welcomed Henry III of France to Venice in 1574.

Benedetto Caliari and Giuseppe Alabardi decorated the two main façades of the Casa Nuova with unusual and particularly well painted frescoes in chiaroscuro. The subjects were Roman stories such as the battle where Ostilio was killed by the Sabines.

In his book La carta del navigar Pittoresco, published in Venice in 1660, Mario Boschini described the entrance yard as beautiful, and figures in the frescoes as looking more real than marble statues and shining like the sun. He wrote that the yard was like a theater telling the greatest triumphs of the ancient Romans when they were the leaders of the universe. These extraordinary frescoes were still visible in the early eighteenth century. Alvise Mocenigo's wife, Loredana Marcello, studied botany with a professor at the famous Botanical Garden of Padua, and it is thought that her love of nature brought another kind of beauty to the Mocenigo courtyard.

The present garden was laid out in the early 1930s. It was decorated with Greek and Roman marbles, and stone sculptures in the Venetian style. Flowering shrubs and vines still cling to the façade, soften the landscape, and provide the cherished shade trees with a very luxuriant setting.

In 1816, the poet Lord Byron arrived in Venice, fell under its spell and moved into an apartment in the Mocenigo Casa Nuova, remaining through 1819. A famous engraving shows him at his desk in a room on the Grand Canal. Today a plaque honors his stay. He was well taken care of by a large staff of servants, and entertained by a menagerie of animals, friends, and mistresses. His days were often filled with strenuous exercise—he wrote

The Mocenigo courtyard has always had a scenic aspect, dating from the time old mulberry trees were moved here from the orchard of the Mocenigo palace in Murano. Now, the doorway to the Casa Nuova is framed with wisteria and oleander. A pair of struggling figures, standing at each side of the opening, add to the drama.

114

of long swims in the Adriatic. Many nights were spent searching for love.

In a letter to John Murray, written November 25, 1816, Lord Byron shared his first impressions:

Venice pleases me as much as I expected, and I expected much. It is one of those places which I know before I see them, and has always haunted me the most after the East. I like the gloomy gaiety of their gondolas, and the silence of their canals . . .

St. Mark's, and indeed Venice, is most alive at night—The theaters are not open til *nine,* and the society is proprotionately late. All of this is to my taste . . .

I have got remarkably good apartments in a private house: I see something of the inhabitants (having had a good many letters to some of them): I have got my gondola; I read a little, and luckily could speak Italian (more fluently though than accurately) long ago. I am studying, out of curiosity, the *Venetian* dialect, which is very naive, and soft, and peculiar, though not at all classical; I go out frequently, and am in very good contentment.

The *Helen* of Canova (a bust which is in the house of Madame the Countess d'Albrizzi, whom I know) is, without exception, to my mind, the most perfectly beautiful of human conceptions, and far beyond my ideas of human execution.

> In this beloved marble view
> Above the works and thoughts of Man,
> What Nature, *could,* but *would not,* do.
> And Beauty and Canova *can!*
> Beyond Imagination's power,
> Beyond the Bard's defeated art,
> With Immortality her dower,
> Behold the *Helen* of the heart.

From Byron's *Beppo: a Venetian story:*

> With all its sinful doings, I must say,
> That Italy's a pleasant place to me,
> Who love to see the Sun shine every day,
> And vines (not nailed to walls) from tree to tree
> Festoon'd, much like the back scene of a play
> Or melodrame, which people flock to see,
> When the first act is ended by a dance
> In vineyards copied from the south of France.

A sampling of plantings in the Mocenigo courtyard: azalea, oleander, asparagus fern, pittosporum, "gold dust" aucuba. A lady holds a shell of greenery high, not realizing she is being observed by a small gentleman.

116

The seventeenth-century Palazzo Dolfin at San Pantalon, now the University of Venice, was famous in the eighteenth century for its collection of Tiepolos commissioned by the family. The garden offers visual delight and the fragrance of roses, jasmine, loquat, and peach.

A classical portal and ornamental iron gates mark the garden entrance to Palazzo Dolfin. Inside is a surprising group of plantings: aspidistra, raphiolepsis, Victorian spiraea, climbing roses, hybrid tea and floribunda roses, crape myrtle, loquat, peach, and a very large banana tree.

The palace at San Pantalon that housed the Dolfins for two centuries—a doge family that also gave the church the leadership of cardinals and bishops—is now filled with the life of the University of Venice. Blooming in the courtyard entrance: wisteria, Japanese aucuba, iris, and jasmine

Palazzo Dolfin at San Pantalon was built for the Secco family and bought by Cardinal Giovanni Dolfin in 1621. Early in the next century, Tiepolo was commissioned to decorate the interior with a number of now-famous paintings that have been scattered to museums in Leningrad, Vienna, and New York.

On February 11, 1709, the Dolfin garden was the site of a gala party for King Frederic IV of Denmark. It was thought that the palace was not large enough for the festivities, so a wooden room, opening into the main rooms on the ground floor, was built in the courtyard. A great assembly of nobility stayed far into the night, dancing, listening to a concert of violins and violas, and admiring the beautiful decorations and candle illuminations. It was during this century that Venetians took to paving over a portion of their gardens to create outdoor rooms. These were often decorated with statues. Goethe in 1786 wrote in his *Italian Journey* of seeing such a courtyard:

In the courtyard of a palazzo, I saw a colossal nude statue of Marcus Agrippa; the wriggling dolphin at his side indicates that he was a naval hero. How true it is that a heroic representation of the human being simply as he is makes him godlike.

He goes on to describe a visit to the Lido:

Now, at last, I have seen the sea with my own eyes and walked upon the beautiful threshing floor of the sand which it leaves behind when it ebbs. . . . Along the shore I found various plants whose common characteristics gave me a better understanding of their individual natures. All are plump and firm, juicy and tough, and it is clear that the salt content of the sand and, even more, the salt in the air is responsible. They are bursting with sap like aquatic plants, yet hardy like mountain flora. The tips of their leaves have a tendency to become prickly like thistles, and when this happens, the spikes grow very long and tough. I found a cluster of such leaves which I took to be our harmless coltsfoot, but it was armed with sharp weapons, and the leaves, the seed capsules and the stalks were as tough as leather. Actually, it was sea holly (*Eryngium maritimum*). I shall bring seeds and pressed leaves with me.

The Dolfin palace was bought and restored during the nineteenth century by the architect G. B. Brusa. Today it houses the University of Venice. The garden contains a varied collection of vines, shrubs, and trees.

Palazzo Savorgnan at San Geremia was built in the late seventeenth century from a plan by architect Giuseppe Sardi. In the nineteenth century the garden was remade in the English style, and was admired for its orchards, pavilions, and sculptures. The garden has been restored by the city of Venice—the first in a series of restoration projects for public gardens.

A classically beautiful building, the symmetry and starkness of Palazzo Savorgnan is set off by the green lawn, the foliage of the venerable trees, and the sparkling water of the fountain.

The city of Venice has restored the generous garden at Palazzo Savorgnan. The palace was built at the end of the seventeenth century for the Savorgnans, who were, according to Giulio Lorenzetti, "the oldest family from the mainland admitted to the Venetian aristocracy in 1385." Now, the manicured lawn, trees, shrubs, and pebbled paths make the garden a pleasant place to walk between the churches of San Giobbe and San Geremia.

The Palazzo Volpi di Misurata is a beautifully restored example of the brilliant style of living in the Republic during the Renaissance. Climbing, swirling, and trailing green vines are surprising and refreshing in the courtyard and add a sense of theater to the setting.

In the courtyard of the Palazzo Volpi di Misurata, beneath grape, English ivy, and Virginia creeper, are classical portals, heroic figures, a historic wellhead, and patterned paving of brick and stone.

Built around the Benedictine church of San Beneto is the large Renaissance Palazzo Volpi di Misurata. Its splendor hides behind a rather serious façade—serious, considering that the entire face to the Grand Canal during the early sixteenth century was covered with a fresco thought at the time to be one of the most spectacular in the city.

The palace, constructed in the sixteenth century for the Talenti family, has passed through several hands. Three of the families—d'Anna, Martinengo, and Volpi di Misurata—contributed greatly to its beauty and preservation. It was Martino d'Anna, a Flemish merchant and art patron, who commissioned the famous fresco from the artist Pordenone. It is said that d'Anna was Titian's godson. Titian was indeed a friend; he painted a portrait of d'Anna, and came often to the palace to see him. In the eighteenth century the house became the property of the patrician Teobaldo Martinengo family, who gave sons and money to defend the Republic, and it remained in their care until the nineteenth century. The present owner is Count Giovanni Volpi di Misurata, the son of Count Giuseppe Volpi di Misurata, who introduced electricity to Venice and served as Italy's Minister of Finance. The family bought the palace in the 1930s and restored it, furnishing and decorating the interior handsomely so that it now has the feeling of the days of the Republic.

There is nothing in the records about a garden, or that one might have existed in the sixteenth century before the palace was extended. Included in Julia Cartwright Ady's book *Italian Gardens of the Renaissance*, however, is a description of an evening with Titian in his garden written by Priscianese, the Roman grammarian:

. . . I was invited to supper in a most beautiful garden, belonging to Messer Tiziano, an excellent painter, as all the world knows . . . The heat of the sun was still great, although the garden is shady, so, while the tables were being carried out and supper laid, we spent our time in looking at the admirable paintings which adorn the house, and in enjoying the rare beauty and delights of the garden, which lies on the sea-shore at the far end of Venice, looking towards the lovely island of Murano and other fair places. As the sun went down, the lagoon swarmed with gondolas full of beautiful women, and the sweet sounds of musical instruments and singing floated over the water and charmed our ears as we sat at our delightful supper till midnight. The garden is beautifully laid out, and excites universal admiration. The supper also was most excellent, rich in choice viands and rare wines. In short, nothing was lacking which could heighten the charm of the summer evening . . .

Grape, English ivy, Virginia creeper, and oleander accentuate the grand scale of the inner courtyard of the Palazzo Volpi di Misurata. Stone figures are copied from finds at Leptis Magna in Libya.

Overleaf: A carefully carved wellhead bears the crest of the Martinengo family. Oleander in flowering season adds color and fragrance to the walls of green.

Second overleaf: Classic stone portals and figures of warriors and gods, in the tradition of the ancient worlds of Rome and Greece, give the courtyard a sense of nobility.

Palazzo Zenobio at Rio
dei Carmini.

Overleaf: *Drawing of
Palazzo Zenobio and its
formal garden by Luca
Carlevaris.*

18th Century

This age of frivolity and fantasy in Venice saw the fanciful rococo embellishment of Gothic and Renaissance architecture. While the works of Tiepolo, Canaletto, Longhi, and Guardi were enriching churches and palaces, a new artistry was also brought to garden design. Gardens were spacious, plans elaborate, and plantings exotic. Stone figures from mythology gave the gardens an aura of history and romance.

ALTRA PARTE D

L' PALAZZO ZENOBIO

Palazzo Zenobio's eighteenth-century garden pavilion, or casino as they are called in Venice, can still be seen today. Tommaso Temanza's design includes Ionic columns, niches for statues, and other classical details. The elaborate pattern of the parterre can only be imagined. Among the more simple plantings: American arborvitae, introduced to Europe in the sixteenth century; clipped laurel; and an assortment of roses.

Overleaf: *Master plan of the ground floor and gardens of Palazzo Zenobio, from the Rubin de Cervin Albrizzi Zenobio archives.*

Palazzo Zenobio was famous in the eighteenth century for its large parterre, laid out in the fashionable French manner. The small casino at the end of the garden was used for entertaining. Its design was unique; a second story contained a family library and archive.

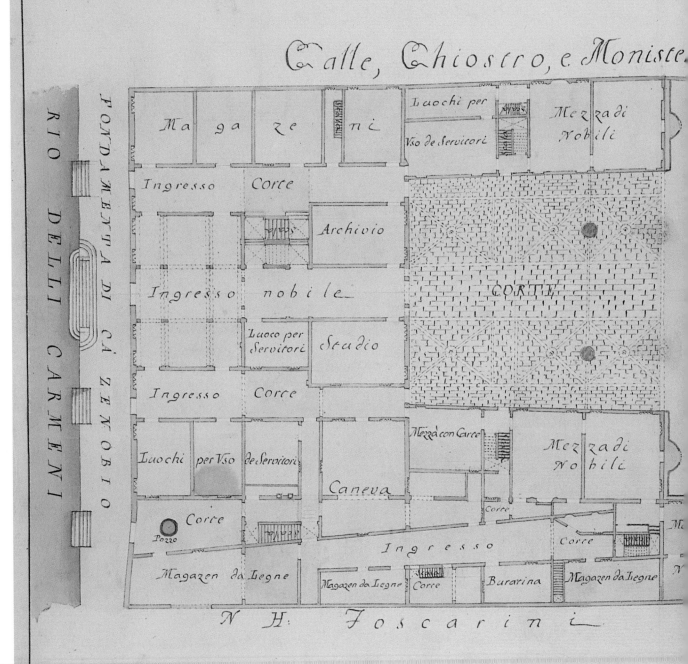

Calle, Chiostro, e Moniste

RIO DELLI CARMENI

FONDAMENTA DI CÁ ZENOBIO

Ma ga ze ni

Luochi per

Vso de Servitori

Mezza di Nobili

Ingresso   Corte

Archivio

Ingresso   nobile

Luoco per Servitori   Studio

CORTE

Ingresso   Corte

Luochi   per Vso   de Servitori

Mezza con Corte

Mezza di Nobili

Caneva

Corte

Corte   Corte

Ingresso

Corte

Pozzo

Magazen da Legne

Magazen da Legne   Corte   Burarina   Magazen da Legne

N. H. Foscarini

PALAZZO DOMINICAL

De RR.PP. Carmelitani

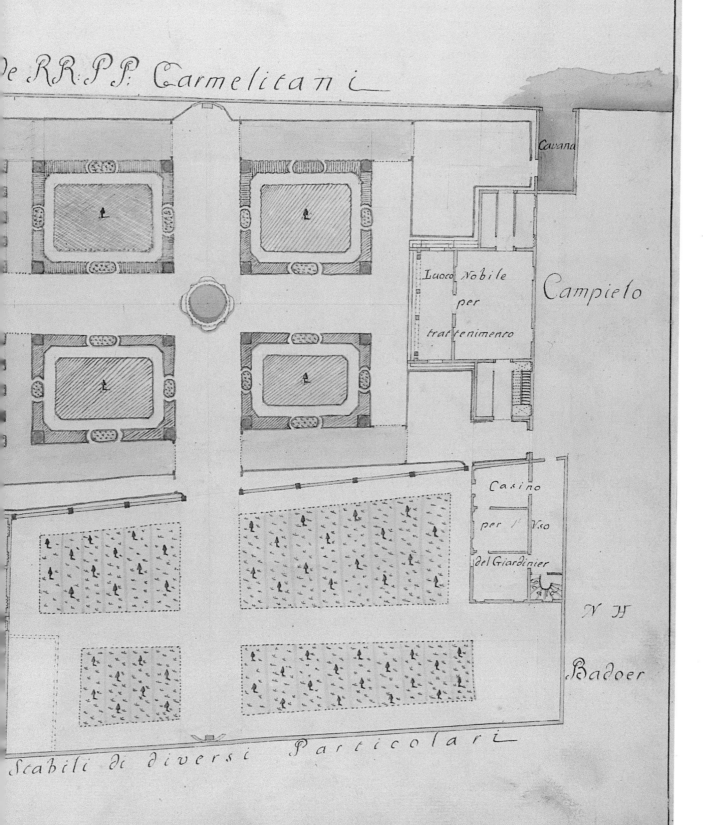

Cavana

Luoco Nobile

per

trattenimento

Campielo

Casino

per l'Vso

del Giardinier

N. H

Badoer

Stabili di diversi Particolari

P art clipped, part wild, the garden at Palazzo Giustiniani Brandolini is an enclosure enveloped in green. Arranged on two levels and presenting two distinct moods, it has a special magic because of its total greenness.

Turks in chains, carved from Istrian stone, stand at the top of the stairs leading to the boxwood garden at Palazzo. Brandolini.

A garden on a starry night is the setting of the second act of *Tristan and Isolde*. The lovers sing of a perfect night of love; a sweet night of eternity. It was in the Palazzo Giustiniani, now Brandolini, at San Barnaba that Richard Wagner set this ancient tale of love and betrayal to music while thinking of his own great passion, Mathilde Wesendonck. He wrote to her on January 19, 1859:

Precisely to the hour, the moment, came your greeting yesterday, as if a neccessity conjured by magic. I was seated at the piano; the old gold pen was spinning its last web over the second act of Tristan, its touch just lingering on the fleeting joys of my pair of lovers' first meeting.

The look and life of Venice, the dramatic Gothic palace where Wagner rented the *mezzanini,* and the gardens where he took his daily walks must all have helped to set the scene, and mood of ecstasy, of his great opera. He described his part of the palace in a letter:

a big drawing room . . . with a . . . splendid mosaic floor, and what is bound to be glorious resonance for the Erard (his piano) . . . The folding doors between the huge bedroom and a little cabinet had to be removed at once, and portières took their place. . . . The color had to be red this time, as the rest of the furniture was that already; only the bedroom is green. An immense hall . . . on one side it has a balcony over the canal, on the other it looks into the courtyard with a little well-paved garden.

Several times Wagner wrote of the haunting call of the gondoliers, his inspiration for the hunting horns that open act two of *Tristan.* He noted in his diary on September 5, 1859:

This night I have been sleepless, long my vigil; my sweet child does not tell me how it fares with her?—Marvellously beautiful, the Canal by night; bright stars, last quarter of the moon. A gondola glides by; from the distance the chant of gondoliers calling to each other. This last is extraordinarily beautiful, sublime . . .

The palace where Wagner lived was built in the fifteenth century by Bartolomeo Bon for the patrician Giustiniani family, and is one of Venice's finest examples of Gothic architecture. Now, in the exuberant spirit of the Gothic façade on the Grand Canal, the courtyard entrance is an explosion of green. The present owner, Count Brandolini d'Adda, shares the interest in gardens of his father, who at the turn of the century introduced many new plants and the small classic garden design. The result is one of the greenest and most surprising gardens in all of Venice.

The varied and intense greens of privet, grape, and a boxwood parterre in the garden of Palazzo Brandolini.

144

At Palazzo Giustiniani Brandolini, raised above the courtyard of Venetian brick, a small garden with clipped boxwood and pebbled paths is a charming reminder of the grand, patterned gardens of the eighteenth century. The surprise is its placement of trees, shrubs, and towering vines in an almost wild setting.

Overleaf: To ensure a feeling of total greenness, Count Brandolini d'Adda encourages the wisteria to climb the façade of the palazzo, and Virginia creeper and English ivy to run rampant over the crenelated garden walls. He makes sure that the yearly pruning does not curtail the vines' enthusiastic coverage of what he considers the less interesting architecture. Two stone angels guard the front gate, and an almost hidden pergola shelters a finely sculpted Roman bath. Scores of different plants thrive in this setting, including oleander, rosemary, acuba "gold dust," Japanese holly, and rhododendron.

P alazzo Gradenigo at
Rio Marin was one of
the most splendid
eighteenth-century
Venetian palaces. The
private park, spacious
enough for stables and
extensive riding paths, was
greatly admired and written
about, and was the scene
of much social life early in
the nineteenth century.

The unusual façade and striking double portal at Palazzo Gradenigo can be seen to advantage from a boat gliding along the Rio Marin. Honeysuckle runs wild on the garden walls.

The very large garden of the Gradenigos at Rio Marin wrapped around their splendid palazzo and extended to the Grand Canal. One of the founding families of the glorious Republic, they gave Venice several doges. The most famous was Pietro, who, in 1297, changed the Republic from a popular democracy to an aristocratic oligarchy of a few Venetian families listed in the "Golden Book," and in 1310 crushed Venice's only internal revolt. It was another Pietro Gradenigo who said "The Republic is dead," when Lodovico Manin, the first doge from the provinces, was elected in 1789. And indeed it was. In 1797 the French arrived, and Manin, Venice's last doge, left in haste, forgetting his crown, to hide in his beautiful villa in the Friuli Region to the north.

The Gradenigo family prospered during the years between these two events. In the eighteenth century the palace was reconstructed from plans by the architect Domenico Margutti, and the city granted permission for the garden to be enlarged to include a portion of a public street. In Napoleon's time the palace was known for its excellent library and superb collection of paintings. Early in the twentieth century, the spacious garden, with its stables and riding paths, was a favorite place for Venetian ladies to gather, to ride, and to show off their new riding costumes. The garden served as the inspiration for the garden of Gabriele d'Annunzio's heroine Foscarina in his novel *The Flame of Youth*.

Although much of the property is now part of Piazzale Roma and its surround, some of the hardier plantings, the walls, the statues, and the noble entrance to the palace tell of the garden's former magnificence.

A Chinese Judas tree provides a rosy backdrop for the stone goddess and child who stand watch. The gate leads into the Gradenigo garden from Campiello della Comare.

Palazzo Soranzo at Rio Marin is a palace of patriarchs and poets, with a garden that inspires all romantics. Large and lush, the garden, now a tangle of ancient trees and vines, is a haunting reminder of the glory of La Serenissima.

A temple portico attached to the back wall of the garden fools the eye. From the palace, the heroic scale of the columns gives the impression of distant grandeur.

The seventeenth-century Palazzo Soranzo at Rio Marin, later belonging to the Bragadin and Cappello families, has retained the immense garden of its youth. Now growing wild, the setting is a fantasy that provokes dreams of past glory. This rare and beautiful place, where Napoleon stayed for a moment, and which Henry James described in the *Aspern Papers,* still has an allure and a certain sense of mystery and adventure.

Henry James expressed his enjoyment and interest in nature in this passage from *The Aspern Papers,* set in the Soranzo Garden:

I made a point of spending as much time as possible in the garden, to justify the picture I had originally given of my horticultural passion. . . . I surveyed the place with a clever expert and made terms for having it put in order. I was sorry to do this, for personally I liked it better as it was, with its weeds and its wild, rough tangle, its sweet, characteristic Venetian shabbiness. I had to be consistent, to keep my promise that I would smother the house in flowers. Moreover I clung to the fond fancy that by flowers I would make my way—I would succeed by big nosegays. I would batter the old women with lilies—I would bombard their citadel with roses. . . . There was a great digging of holes and carting about of earth, and after a while I grew so impatient that I had thoughts of sending for my bouquets to the nearest stand. . . . So I composed myself and finally, though the delay was long, perceived some appearances of bloom. This encouraged me and I waited serenely enough till they multiplied. Meanwhile the real summer days arrived and began to pass, and as I look back upon them they seem to me almost the happiest of my life. I took more and more care to be in the garden whenever it was not too hot. I had an arbour arranged and a low table and an armchair put into it; and I carried out books and portfolios—I had always some business of writing in hand—and worked and waited and mused and hoped, while the golden hours elapsed and the plants drank in the light and the inscrutable old palace turned pale and then, as the day waned, began to flush and my papers rustled in the wandering breeze of the Adriatic.

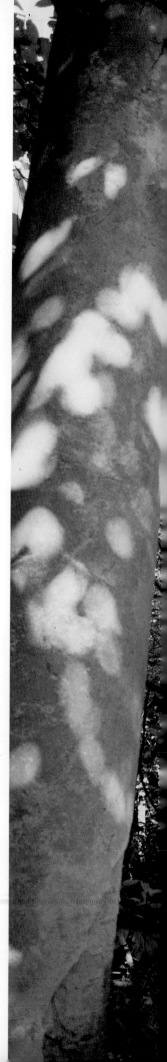

The garden temple at Palazzo Soranzo might have been intended for more than just the delight of the eye. It would have been a romantic setting for a moonlit rendezvous or a midnight supper party.

Overleaf: *Engraving of Palazzo Soranzo and its well-planned garden,* by the Venetian cartographer Father Vincenzo Coronelli.

PALAZZO S.
IN
RIO MARI

Four of twelve Caesars in the garden at Palazzo Soranzo. They stand in niches in the walls of the garden enclosure next to the palace. Part of the classical design of the garden, the Caesars pay homage to Roman history.

Overleaf: The path into the garden from the center door of the palace. A pair of struggling figures depict the rape of the Sabine women. Some of the plantings that remain: a laurel hedge, oleander, palms, and Japanese fatsia.

The Papadópoli
Gardens at Piazzale
Roma

Overleaf: Drawing of
the Public Garden on
Riva degli Schiavoni

19th Century

This was the century of the public garden, part of Napoleon's legacy to Venice. The patricians retired to their country villas, but as the century progressed their city gardens came under the spell of the classical revival, perhaps inspired by the drawings of Piranesi and the sculpture of Canova. More figures and fragments from excavations appeared, so that some gardens became gardens of art.

G. Borsato dis.

Entrée aux I

F. Juliani inc.

rdins public

For Venice, The Public Garden, a garden of triumph for Napoleon, and the Papadópoli Garden, a garden of neighborly love, are generous expanses of nature and lasting gifts to the citizens of the city.

This great stone portal, an entrance to nowhere, stands alone in the Public Garden as a reminder of the churches that were leveled to make way for Napoleon's garden. The portal was once part of the chapel of the Sandi family in the Church of Sant' Antonio. Saved from destruction but abandoned, it was rediscovered, restored, and put into place in 1922.

A mark of Napoleon's triumph over Venice is the public garden he had designed for *all* the people. Its creation was a well-aimed blow to the patricians and the social structure of the Republic. This grand gesture unfortunately called for the tearing down of churches and small houses of fishermen and lacemakers in the colorful Castello area. The architect chosen for the project was Gian Antonio Selva, the respected designer of such buildings as the first Fenice Theater. His original plan, since altered, called for a design of simple beauty. Traces can be seen in the entrance, a curved iron fence, punctuated by stone pillars topped with impressive stone figures. A noble Venetian, Pier Antonio Zorzi, a scholar and horticulturalist, selected and supervised the plantings.

The garden opened in 1810 to much acclaim, and continues to serve Venetians as a place for picnics, promenades, and celebrations. Since 1895, the garden has been known for the now-famous Biennale, an international art exhibition. Some twenty pavilions stand in the heart of the garden, and are used by visiting nations to show the works of their artists. Lofty plane trees and poplars make it a cool and pleasant place to be on a warm summer's day.

Soon to follow was another public garden, Papadópoli, an unexpected sun screen of leafy green enroute from the Tolentini Bridge to the Piazzale Roma. Planted in ancient convent walls, tall tree branches make a lacy canopy over paths leading to the Grand Canal.

In the mid-nineteenth century, the Papadópoli gardens, lush with rare flowers and trees, drew Venetians to view the beauty and enjoy festivals that filled the night. Picturesque arrangements of water, plantings and paths, very English in feeling, with gazelles and pheasants romping in almost natural habitats, were a great attraction when the garden first opened in 1834. The garden was the inspiration of Count Spiridione Papadópoli, who assembled several properties and commissioned the painter-landscape architect Francesco Bagnara to make a splendid garden. In 1863, the garden was remade from plans by French garden designer Marc Guignon. Visitors can now only dream of the garden's glory as they pause for refreshment in the shade.

Napoleon's Public Gardens are home for a number of stone statues of history and myth. Many were brought here from the Villa Pisani in Strà. During the eighteenth century, families of stonecutters were rich with commissions for heroes from the ancient worlds—saints, gods, godesses, or simply romantic figures—that would add beauty and drama to architecture and its landscape. Here, a classic figure appears triumphant on the back of a kingly lion.

Overleaf: *In a shady setting of mature trees and shrubs—among them, grey-leaf poplar, Chinese mulberry, purple-leaf plum, Japanese aucuba, and laurel pruned in different ways—one beauty does not go unnoticed.*

The nineteenth-century
garden of the sixteenth-
century Palazzzo Nani
Lucheschi has a hint of the
neo-classic in its attitude,
and a touch of the tropics
in its plantings. The palace,
much smaller in scale when
compared to its neighbor
Ca'Rezzonico, has one of
the largest gardens in
Venice.

*In the garden of
Countess Maria
Lucheschi Czarnocki tall
palmettos are set in a
formal arrangement.
Panels of lawn, pebbled
paths, and beds of
hybrid tea roses are
bordered with clipped
Japanese boxwood.*

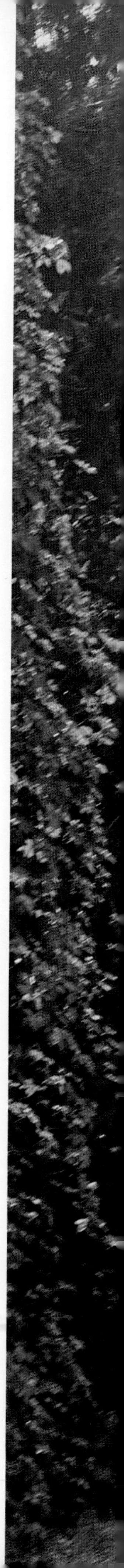

Left: *Looking toward the pergola at the back of Palazzo Nani Lucheschi, iris and a floribunda rose suggest the variety in the plantings. Also visible is the very tall mature palmetto, the palm of Palm Sunday.*

Right: *In the pergola, the twisted trunk of an ancient wisteria. Its generous coverage of fresh green and palest purple has been going on for decades. Adding to the shade: an evergreen, glossy leaved fatshedera.*

While Venice began the nineteenth century as the city of Napoleon, and the Austrians, it was later the Venice of George Sand, the Ruskins, Whistler, and Henry James, who saw it freshly through artists' eyes.

In a letter written from Venice dated April 1834, published in *Lettres d'un Voyageur*, George Sand shares her deep feelings for the city:

My friend, you have no idea of what Venice is. . . . At present, spring has breathed upon her, as though her breath were emerald dust. The base of her palaces, where oysters clustered in the stagnant moss, is now covered with the most tender green, and gondolas float between two banks of this verdure, soft as velvet, and the noise of the water dies away languishingly, mingled with the foam of the gondola's track.

When the breath of midnight passes over the linden trees, and scatters their blossoms over the waters, when the perfume of wallflowers and geraniums rises in gusts, as though the earth gave forth her sighs of fragrance to the moon; when the cupolas of Santa Maria raise towards heaven their alabaster hemispheres and their turban-crowned minarets; when all is white, the water, the sky, the marble, the three elements of Venice, and when from the tower of St. Mark's a giant sound hovers over my head, then I begin to feel life through every pore . . .

Venice's climate is kind to trees and shrubs that live in a subtropical atmosphere, and to many of the bulbs and flowering bushes native to northern climates. The garden at Palazzo Nani Lucheschi is a well-planned and well-tended example of this versatility. Plantings include laurel and Japanese aucuba allowed to go native, combined with precisely clipped boxwood in a decorative pattern.

Unexpected on the Grand Canal, the very green and colorful garden at Palazzo Malipiero Barnabò is a stage for allegorical figures by some of Venice's great stonecutters. They tell a story of a time and place, and of many lives.

The owners of Palazzo Cappello Malipiero, the Alessandro Barnabò family, take much pleasure in the design of their garden. Two symbols of Venice's kinship to the sea, Neptune in his temple and the boy with a dolphin, are placed in an ornamental arrangement of beds of hybrid tea roses contained in low boxwood hedges. Laurel and Japanese aucuba are visible in the background.

Palazzo Malipiero Barnabò at San Samuele, a thirteenth-century building reconstructed during the seventeenth century, was part of the dowry of Elisabetta Cappello to her husband Cattarin Malipiero, and some say it is their likenesses that are carved on the wellhead that stands in the garden. When the palace was restored in the nineteenth century, the garden took shape. Covering the space once occupied by a smaller house, it flows to the edge of the Grand Canal. The parterre and the formal way stone figures are displayed are typical of the period. In addition to Neptune in his temple and the boy with a dolphin, there are four allegorical figures by the sculptor Antonio Bonazza: a digger, representing Spring; a flutist, as Summer; a seated figure with a sickle, depicting Autumn; and a bagpipe player, representing Winter. These figures add romance and excitement to a garden already bursting with flowering bushes, rampant vines, and clipped green borders. The garden is a wonder and a delight to all who pass along the canal.

The predominance of architecture and water in Venice seem to make all gardens there unexpected. In *Italian Hours*, Henry James wrote:

I am on firm ground in rejoicing in the little garden directly opposite our windows—it is another proof that they really show us everything—and in feeling that the gardens of Venice would deserve a page to themselves. They are infinitely more numerous than the arriving stranger can suppose; they nestle with a charm all their own in the complications of most back views. Some of them are exquisite, many are large, and even the scrappiest have an artful understanding, in the interest of colour, with the waterways that edge their foundations. On the small canals, in the hunt for amusement, they are the prettiest surprises of all. The tangle of plants and flowers crowds over the battered walls, the greenness makes an arrangement with the rosy sordid brick. Of all the reflected and liquefied things in Venice, and the number of these is countless, I think the lapping water loves them most. They are numerous on the Canalazzo, but wherever they occur they give a brush to the picture and in particular, it is easy to guess, give a sweetness to the house. Then the elements are complete—the trio of air and water and of things that grow. Venice without them would be too much a matter of the tides and the stones. . . .

At Palazzo Malipiero Barnabò, allegorical stone figures add meaning and character to the parterre garden—Neptune in his temple; the digger as Spring, on the far left; and the flutist, representing Summer, on the far right.

Overleaf: *Seen in the foreground, a collection of hybrid tea roses, a sweep of Virginia creeper, and a weeping cedar. The wellhead is said to be carved with the faces of a Cappello and a Malipiero.*

Second overleaf: *A close-up of the flutist of spring by Antonio Bonazza, one of a prolific family of artists who filled Venice's churches, palaces, and gardens during the eighteenth century. Evergreen euonymus covers a pergola sheltering a romantic stone figure of a young woman.*

Over the Albrizzi bridge and into the garden below—a most surprising entrance to a Venetian garden that is the pleasing result of almost two hundred years of one family's love for their garden and plant collecting. Its romantic beginnings inspired the plan for its current restoration.

High above the Rio San Cassiano a slender bridge connects the piano nobile of Palazzo Albrizzi to a neo-Gothic tower and a stair that spirals to the garden below. The garden was the creation of Nobildonna Alba Zenobio Albrizzi in the early nineteenth century.

There are two main entrances to the Albrizzi garden: the bridge and tower leading from the palazzo, and the gate from Rio San Cassiano. The plantings are a fascinating collection of international origin, including phormium, a green fiber lily native to New Zealand; ornamental European dune grass; laurel, cultivated by the ancient Greeks and Romans; and Japanese dwarf lilyturf, which lines paths and plant beds.

In the late eighteenth century more than one hundred performing theaters, opera houses, and casinos made life very entertaining for rich Venetians. The Teatro San Cassiano, just across the Rio San Cassiano from Palazzo Albrizzi, is said to have been one of the first public opera houses in Europe. The opera house was built in 1636; it opened the next year with *Andromeda* written by Benedetto Ferrari with music by Francesco Manelli. The adjacent casino, famous for dinner parties at intermission and after theater, was a favorite of pleasure-loving Venetians.

Napoleon's conquest brought a great age of enjoyment to an end. The new ideas of liberty and equality and the loss of privileges for the patricians caused the noble families to retreat to their country estates, slowing down the life of the city. Theaters closed and fell into decay, prompting the new government to call for their destruction. Theater sites began to change hands and character.

In 1812, the San Cassiano theater property was transferred from the textile-rich Tron family to the Cameranovics, Dalmatians in the business of shipping between Venice and Split. When the Albrizzi family bought the land in 1820, a ten-foot-high wall was all that remained of the theater that had once throbbed with life.

Nobildonna Alba Zenobio Albrizzi had dreams of a garden of shade and seclusion, but as she attempted to reconstruct the garden wall, the family was immediately sued by actor Pietro Roggia, tenant of the little casino house just to the East. The suit was soon settled: the Procuratessa Albrizzi built her wall; Roggia received a handsome sum of money.

The powerful Zenobio family owned land from Verona to the Tyrol as well as some 140 properties in Venice. Alba herself was owner of the celebrated Palazzo Zenobio at the Carmini, with its extraordinarily beautiful garden. Documents in the Museo Correr show that in 1833 she called in Gian Battista Meduna, the architect who rebuilt the facade of Teatro la Fenice, to do an architectural survey of the Albrizzi garden. He described the garden as "majestic and aristocratic." Another drawing of the garden in the Albrizzi family archives is signed by Meduna and dated 1862. There is speculation, but no proof, that Meduna may have designed the unusual neo-Gothic tower that links the garden to the palazzo.

In the late nineteenth century, Elsa de' Margarit Albrizzi was the contessa in residence at Palazzo Albrizzi. In his book *Gondola Days*, published in 1897, the author and illustrator F. Hopkinson Smith described most vividly a visit to the contessa's garden. Although "the *Illustrissima* was then sojourning at her country-seat in the Tyrol," a viewing was arranged by his friend Professor Croisac.

The sound of water splashing from a small fountain, and the shimmer of goldfish in a rock-rimmed pool add to the pleasure of the Albrizzi garden. Sword ferns are planted among the rocks. In the surroundings: A semi-bonsaied oak; a Japanese thorny elaeagnus; a magnolia, native to the southern United States; an American yucca; and a bergenia, native to Siberia.

"And all for two *lire* to the porter on duty," Smith related. He further wrote:

First of all I must see the gorgeous ceilings of the Albrizzi; then the curious vine-covered bridge leading out of the Contessa's boudoir to a garden across the narrow canal, as secluded as the groves of Eden before Adam stepped into them. . . .

. . . look at the grand hall, with its sides a continuous line of pictures! Its ceiling a marvel of stucco and rich-colored canvases! Do you find anything like this outside of Venice? And now come through the salon, all white and gold, to the bridge spanning the canal. Here, you see, is where my lady steps across and so down into her garden when she would be alone. You must admit that this is quite unique.

The Professor was right. A bridge from a boudoir to a garden wall, sixty or more feet above the water-line, is unusual, even in Venice.

And such a bridge! All smothered in vines, threading their way in and out the iron lattice-work of the construction, and sending their tendrils swinging, heads down, like acrobats, to the water below. And such a garden! Framed in by high prison walls, their tops patrolled by sentinels of stealthy creepers and wide-eyed morning-glories! A garden with a little glass-covered arbor in the centre plot, holding a tiny figure of the Virgin; circular stone benches for two, *and no more*; tree- trunks twisted into seats, with encircling branches for shoulders and back, and all, too, a thousand miles in the wilderness for anything you could hear or see of the life of the great city about you. A garden for lovers and intrigues and secret plots, and muffled figures smuggled through mysterious water-gates, and stolen whisperings in the soft summer night. A garden so utterly shut in, and so entirely shut out, that the daughter of a Doge could take her morning bath in the fountain with all the privacy of a boudoir.

'Yes,' said the Professor, with a slight twinkle in his eye, 'these old Venetians knew; and perhaps some of the modern ones.'

The Albrizzi garden, first conceived in the early nineteenth century, was lush with plantings in the style of the English gardens of the period. Each succeeding generation cared for the garden, adding to it and changing it slightly with the fashion of the times. In keeping with the spirit of restoration in Venice, Baron Alessandro Rubin de Cervin Albrizzi, the present owner, recently commissioned landscape architect Bruce Kelly to make a plan for the renewal of the garden. His challenge was to recapture some of the feeling of Alba Zenobio Albrizzi's original plan, retaining and encouraging as much of the old plant life as possible. Work began in 1985.

What Bruce Kelly found in the old garden inspired him:

The range of plants is extraordinary for their origin and ages. There are plants from Europe, Asia, Africa, and North America; plants a hundred years old, seventy-five years old, fifty years old, two years old. The garden represents six generations of development, enrichment, and contribution—plus changing attitudes toward gardening, from nineteenth-century plant collecting to modern mixed borders.

The rage for plant collecting in the last century brought an unexpected variety of plants to the Albrizzi garden. Trees and shrubs of many nations now thrive there: a linden from Berlin; purple-leaved plum, introduced from Persia in 1880; English yew; American elm; European weeping beech; Japanese pittosporum; Chinese crape myrtle; variegated Siberian dogwood; and St. John's-wart, developed at Hidcote Manor Garden, Gloucestershire, England.

Many ornamental plants give a great change of shape, leaf, and color to the garden: Japanese aucuba, fatshedera, euonymus, pyracantha, cotoneaster, European forsythia, native lavender and rosemary, English ivy, and an abundance of Virginia creeper that covers walls with summer green and autumn red. All of these create a pleasing experience as the path from the tower steps leads deep into the property, and back to the canal gate. Architectural fragments from the Albrizzi villa in the Veneto, placed along the way, add beauty to the walk and hint of the splendor of ancient worlds.

The plan for the Albrizzi restoration emphasizes the garden's superb collection of plantings, with winding paths for promenades to enjoy their artful placement.

Overleaf: *The Albrizzi garden occupies a refreshing half-acre of leafy green where the Rio di San Cassiano and the Rio della Madonnetta meet on their way to the Grand Canal. If a gondola pauses at the old iron gate its passengers will see a romantic pergola covered with Chinese wisteria, and a garden that includes trees, shrubs, and flowers gathered from all over the world.*

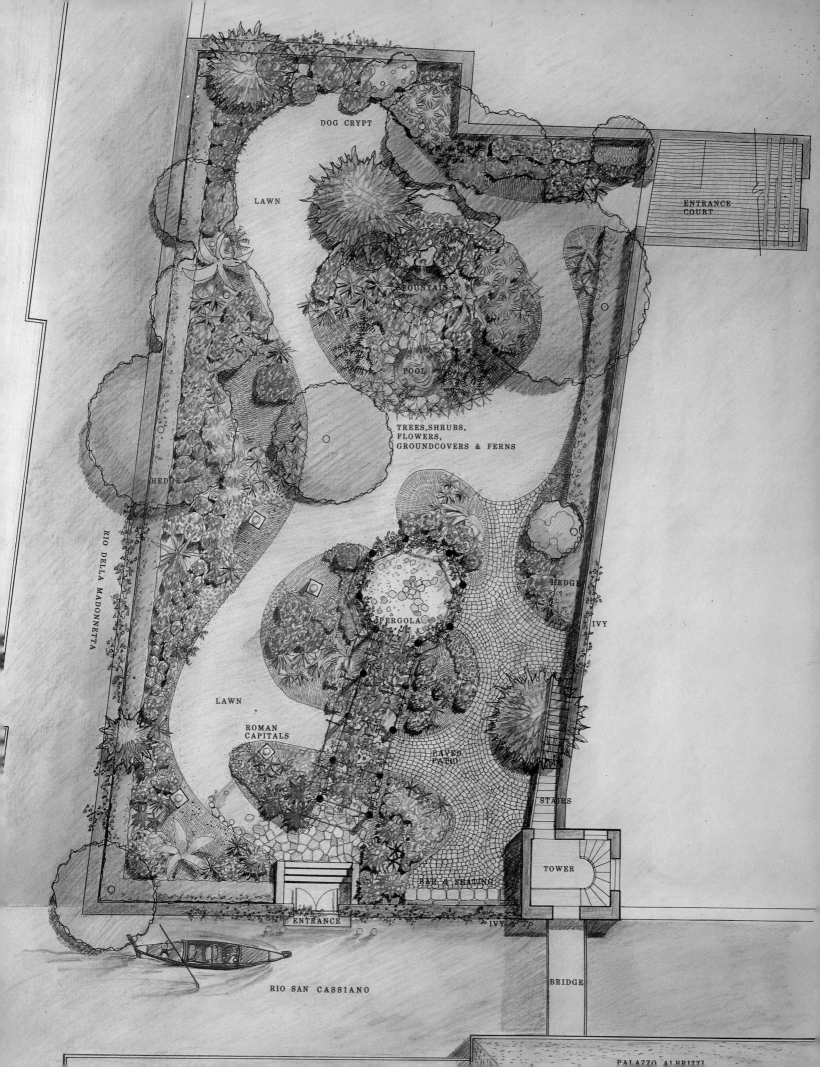

ENTRANCE
COURT

DOG CRYPT

LAWN

FOUNTAIN

POOL

TREES, SHRUBS,
FLOWERS,
GROUNDCOVERS & FERNS

HEDGE

RIO DELLA MADONNETTA

HEDGE

IVY

PERGOLA

LAWN

ROMAN
CAPITALS

PAVED
PATIO

STAIRS

TOWER

BAR & SEATING

ENTRANCE

IVY

RIO SAN CASSIANO

BRIDGE

PALAZZO ALBRIZZI

Casetta Rossa, with the campanile of San Stefano in the background.

Overleaf: Casetta Rossa photographed from the terrace of the Guggenheim foundation.

20th Century

Since the turn of the century, Venice has been an important center for culture, with festivals and exhibitions of art, architecture, theater, opera, music, and films. Two world wars have directed the city's energies to reconstruction and restoration. Public and private gardens are undergoing vigorous rejuvenation. The renewal of the Island of San Giorgio has led the way. Today, Venice is a meeting place of nations for the benefit of all mankind.

N amed for its roses and painted a rosy red, the Casetta Rossa is a small house, with its own garden on the Grand Canal, that has echoed with the laughter and sighs of some of the twentieth century's most interesting visitors to Venice.

Virginia creeper covers the rosy facade of Casetta Rossa. The pomegranate tree, planted by Gabriele d'Annunzio during the First World War, still flourishes in the garden which now belongs to Evelina Levi Broglio.

IO HO QVEL CHE HO DONATO

Mia cara amica,

iersera speravo d'incontrarla a San Vidal tra gli spiriti della melodia.

Ecco cinquanta esemplari del mio piccolo libro di fede pei Suoi feriti e infermi.

Vuol venire stasera a pranzo nella Casa rossa — alle 8 e 1/4?

Se sì, posso mandarLe la gondola che è sempre alla mia riva.

Sì?

Gabriele d'Annunzio

The small red house, Casetta Rossa, tucked in a row of great palaces, is always a surprise to visitors as they boat along the Grand Canal. It stands close to Palazzo Barbaro, separated only by a small green space once occupied by the studio of the sculptor Canova. A charming contrast to its towering neighbors, Casetta Rossa, named for its rose garden, was built at the turn of the century for Prince Frederich Hohenlohe by the architect Rupolo. The Venetian-born prince, a member of the Austrian Hohenlohe family and a diplomat, retired to his little red house until the outbreak of the First World War.

In 1915, the colorful Gabriele d'Annunzio, novelist, poet, playwright, and war hero, rented the Casetta Rossa. It was an ideal place to recover from wounds he sustained when his plane crashed on January 16, 1916. His war exploits were much publicized, and although almost blinded, he led a very productive and social convalescence in the little red house until 1918. Venice was intoxicating to him and its headiness permeated his writings. *Notturno* was written during his stay at Casetta Rossa. The attractive house and delightful garden were a perfect setting for receiving friends, and helped to restore his sight and creative zeal.

During his stay at the Casetta Rossa, writer d'Annunzio hastened his convalescence from war wounds with dinner parties and other entertainments. This invitation to Countess Albrizzi is written on letter paper he designed himself, imprinted with one of several dramatic drawings that he used to enliven his correspondence.

Gabriele d'Annunzio was a man of great passion. His many loves fill his writings, provoking strong emotions. Much has been written about his liaison with actress Eleònora Duse—they met in Venice in 1894—including his own novel, *Il Fuoco (The Flame of Life)*, published in 1900. In his biography, *d'Annunzio,* Tommaso Antongini wrote: "I myself saw her on two occasions correcting fragments of *Il Fuoco,* and have reason to believe that these occasions were by no means exceptional."

Surprising, for the story mirrors d'Annunzio and Duse's life together—a young poet in love with an older actress, who, suffering for her lost youth and fearing rejection, leaves him. The baroque appearance and life of Venice set the scene for the book—the Cappello palace and the Gradenigo garden are home in the novel to the actress La Foscarina. D'Annunzio describes her visit to a garden on the Giudecca, a garden that must have been inspired by the one belonging to Englishman F. Eden, in this way:

She came out by the wharf, stepped into a gondola, had herself rowed to the island of Giudecca. The harbor, the Salute Church, the Riva degli Schiavoni, all the stone and all the water, were a miracle of gold and opal. . . .

She was in the Rio della Croce. The foliage grew above the red wall. The gondola stopped at a closed door. She landed, took out a small key, opened the door, and went into the garden.

It was her refuge, the secret place of her solitude, preserved by her faithful melancholies as by silent custodians. All came forward to meet her, the old ones and the new ones, surrounded her, accompanied her.

With its long trellises, with its cypresses, with its fruit-trees, with its edges of lavender, its oleanders, its carnations, its rose-bushes crimson and crocus colored, marvelously soft and tired in the colors of its dissolution, that garden seemed lost in the extreme lagoon, on one of those islands forgotten by man, Mazzorbo, Torcello, San Francesco del Deserto. The sun embraced it and penetrated it on every side so that the shadows were so slight as to be hardly visible; so great was the stillness of the air that the dry vine leaves stayed on their tendrils. None of the leaves fell; though all were dead.

Arriving at the Casetta Rossa by gondola, one strolls through the small front garden to reach the house. The pergola of vines at water's edge, and along the side of the garden, offers shade and shelter enroute to the door. Well situated on the Grand Canal, this garden is a pleasant place to receive guests, watch the boat life, and sense the changing of tempos of the city.

Over the rooftops of Venice, the *altane*, a Venetian creation, wait to catch the sun, the stars, and the breezes from the sea. At Palazzo da Mula terraces and *altane* are a garden with a spectacular view.

Virginia creeper in the brilliant scarlet autumn coloration. Beyond the winged lion on the chimney, looking to the southeast, the bell tower of San Marco and the restoration of Palazzo Fini.

The altane *and terraces connecting on several levels at Palazzo da Mula are the creation of the antiquarian Franco Lombardi. Embellishments include statues and architectural fragments from his collection and Venetian-style lanterns. The trellis covering of Virginia creeper provides this potted garden with dramatic seasonal changes of color. The view to the northwest is toward the Accademia Bridge.*

During the sixteenth century courtesans sought the sun on rooftop *altane,* the wooden platforms with spidery frames that give Venice its distinctive skeletal skyline. Some say the *altane* were designed especially for those Venetian beauties, and were the secret of their famous golden tresses so often seen in paintings. Behind drawn curtains the courtesans took advantage of the oldest beauty treatment in the world—the sun. While their complexions were protected under wide-brimmed straw hats, their hair would be pulled through the open crowns and spread out on the brims to catch the brightening effects of the sun. Venice still reaches to the sun from these rooftop terraces.

Today, some *altane* have been transformed into gardens in the sky, such as the one created by Franco Lombardi at Palazzo da Mula. A series of terraces, connecting *altane* on several levels, crown this venerable palazzo on the Grand Canal at San Vio. It is a place to sun, and even better, a place to catch the first evening breeze and a spectacular view of the city. It is a pergola in the sky for a dinner close to the stars, and a superb vantage point on a brilliant night of fireworks.

The Countess Annina Morosini, a great beauty of this century, lived at Palazzo da Mula. She was the daughter of banker Rombo of Genoa who married into the illustrious Morosini family of Venice. It was Count Morosini's colorful and fearless ancestor, the Doge Francesco Morosini, who conquered the whole of the Peloponnesus for Venice in the seventeenth century. It is written that he wore nothing but red and always sailed into battle with his cat beside him. Annina Morosini, reported to be the most beautiful woman in Europe, was painted by many famous painters of the day, including Boldini. Hearing of her great beauty, Kaiser Wilhelm came to Venice especially to see her. There is a postcard, prized by collectors, showing his arrival at her door on March 26, 1908. His visit caused a scandal that Venetians still talk about, while describing her charms with admiration and pride.

T
he Institute of Architecture of the University of Venice, in the monastery of the church of San Nicolò da Tolentino, is an example of the harmony of church and school in sixteenth-century and twentieth-century architectural terms. The entrance and garden are based on an idea of the poetical artist-designer Carlo Scarpa.

Angles against arches and cement against brick at the Institute of Architecture of the University of Venice and the church of San Nicolò da Tolentino. These two architectural expressions, with four centuries between them, send clear signals of the intent of the institutions. Together they dramatize the purpose of each.

The church of San Nicolò da Tolentino and its adjoining monastery were built between 1591 and 1602 by the architect Vincenzo Scamozzi on property assembled by San Gaetano da Thiene for the Teatini Friars. The interior plan is said to have been somewhat revised by Palladio, who may had added to its classical grandeur. Richly decorated with chapels dedicated to some of Venice's most patrician families—the Pisani, Soranzo, and Grimani, among others—the church offers much to be admired. The newer classical facade, with a grand Corinthian vestibule by Andrea Tiral, was built in the early eighteenth century. Located in a well-traveled part of the city the church can be reached via the Tolentini bridge.

The church monastery, unused for its original purpose since Napoleon's time, has been taken on by the University of Venice and reconstructed to suit the needs of its Institute of Architecture. The entrance gate and garden, planned in 1975, are based on an idea of the renowned designer Carlo Scarpa, a Venetian associated with the university for some fifty years.

The entrance wall of angles and levels of cement and the sliding gate of glass tell the passerby that this is a place of this century, and beckons one to see what is beyond. The surprise and wonder of the small inner space is the reflecting pool sculpted around a great marble portal from the old church.

A large, ancient stone portal from the church of San Nicolò da Tolentino is at the center of the sculpted reflecting pool, a provocative detail of the entrance garden at the Institute of Architecture of the University of Venice. The tree is a Southern magnolia.

Carlo Scarpa, Director of the Institute of Architecture between 1972 and 1975, gave Venice two most interesting twentieth-century gardens—the entrance to the Institute and the garden at the Querini-Stampalia Foundation. Both are based on strong Venetian traditions, but enriched with the worldly influences this modern artist-designer brought back to his much-loved city of birth. Scarpa felt the brilliance of Gaudi, Le Corbusier, Frank Lloyd Wright, and Louis Kahn. He had a great affinity for Japan, and the simplicity and purity of Japanese design is strongly sensed in many of his international projects. His early studies were classical and he said he had been educated "between Byzantium and Greece."

The changing light and colors, the abundance of water, and the scarcity of land in Venice were all elements of design to Scarpa. He used the great craft traditions of the city, based on glass, wood, metal, and stone to give the texture and contour to his work that is so surprising and rewarding. In the gardens, the green of nature was added with a bold stroke, and like the other elements, was not left uncontrolled. In *GA Document*, Philip Johnson once said: "Carlo Scarpa was the leading architect in details of modern times and could make poetry out of the smallest rod or piece of stone. . . . No one with this kind of genius is left today."

Carlo Scarpa liked everything horizontal, such as the sea, and his Venice gardens are based on strong horizontal planes. At the Institute of Architecture, the reflecting pool, set in an old stone portal, is a composition of steps and angles. Opposite, a Southern magnolia grows in a contained panel of lawn grass.

Overleaf: The modern materials of the coutryard garden are in harmony with the old monastery building. English ivy and Virginia creeper climb the walls. The hand of Le Corbusier marks the entrance door.

Palazzo Venier dei Leoni, now the home of the Peggy Guggenheim Foundation, is a palace of paintings and a garden of sculpture that delivers a universal message. It is a place where a very personal collection of twentieth-century art takes its place in history.

The Angel of the Citadel by Marino Marini from the Peggy Guggenheim collection at Palazzo Venier dei Leoni. English ivy and red salvia decorate the handsome iron gates that open on to the Grand Canal.

Palazzo Venier dei Leoni, named for one of Venice's oldest and most distinguished families, and now the home of the Peggy Guggenheim Foundation, gained much of its fame from three women recently drawn to Venice. First, the Comtesse de la Baume-Pluvinel, who rescued the partially-built palace from its life as a *pensione*, and used it as a guest house and a place for entertainments when she lived at Palazzo Dario. Second was the exotic Marchesa Casati, who kept a leopard in her garden and gathered a group of eccentric friends around her. Dressed in masquerade costumes they walked the leopard in Piazza San Marco followed by hundreds of laughing children. In 1951, Peggy Guggenheim bought the palace as a home for herself and her remarkable collection of twentieth-century paintings and sculpture.

If Palazzo Venier dei Leoni had been completed from the plans presented to the family in 1749 by the architect Lorenzo Boschetti, it would have been one of the most splendid on the Grand Canal, even larger and more magnificent than Palazzo Rezzonico. For whatever reason, the palace was never finished, so that now this long, low structure, almost hidden in volumes of vines and trees, makes a startling appearance in contrast to its neighbors. Inside, the two ground floors of the projected palace—unadorned and smaller in scale than the planned *piani nobili*—are most sympathetic to the Guggenheim collection of art of this century.

The Venier family gave Venice three doges, eighteen procurators, and many brave military men. Following the Venetian custom of various branches of a family adopting a second name that tells of their interests or exploits, this branch of the Venier family took the name "dei Leoni." It is said that they kept a lion in their garden, and the giant lion heads in the stone base overhanging the canal add to this legend.

English ivy covers the stone pergola in the garden of the Peggy Guggenheim Foundation. The stone is carved with flowers and clusters of grapes. The sides of the pergola form seats for the large stone table at its center. The garden has recently been laid out by the architect Giorgio Bellavitis.

Overleaf, left: Pittosporum, oleander, and a canopy of loquat shade important pieces of sculpture: in the foreground, Chinese Dog 2 by Eduardo Paolozzi; to the right, Tauromachie by Germaine Richier.

Overleaf, right: Virginia creeper surrounds Architectural Element—Lines of Force in Space by Mirko Basaldella. The entrance gate was made by Claire Falkenstein.

As a child, Peggy Guggenheim often visited Europe with her family. Her early study of Italian Renaissance art introduced her to the art of Venice and the allure of the city, and helped prepare her for the later role of art patron and collector. For the last twenty-eight years of her life she lived in Venice in the Palazzo Venier dei Leoni, a surprising, but extremely complementary background for her very personal collection of paintings and sculpture.

Venice, a center for art and artists through the ages, welcomed this visionary art patron, and respected and honored her in many ways. Her passion for the art of her time has given the world the Peggy Guggenheim Foundation, and the rare opportunity of seeing some two hundred examples of Dada, Suprematist, Cubist, and Surrealist art, among other works, in a spectacular setting.

Palazzo Venier dei Leoni, an unfinished palace that once held such glittering promise, has found its destiny in the art of the twentieth century.

The rooftop terrace at Palazzo Venier dei Leoni, now the Peggy Guggenheim Foundation, offers a great vantage point to view life on the Grand Canal. The superb view here is toward the church of La Salute, the lagoon, and Piazza San Marco.

All Venice gardens are distilled into one at the Querini-Stampalia Foundation, a "perfect" work of the modern master Carlo Scarpa. Here, nature's most rewarding materials are brought together with great finesse and feeling.

Ancient artifacts against modern blocks of stone in the small enclosed garden at the Querini-Stampalia Foundation. English ivy clings to the high brick walls and creates a green horizon for the old palazzo. The level of the lawn and the other plantings is raised like a theater stage—a stroke of showmanship that adds greatly to the garden's interest.

Palazzo Querini-Stampalia, now the Querini-Stampalia Foundation, is a massive, elegant Renaissance-style building dating from the sixteenth century. It was the home of the patrician Querini-Stampalia family who figured prominently in the affairs of the Republic for three centuries. Following the Venetian custom of adopting names of conquered territory, this branch of the Querini family added the name Stampalia after seizing the Aegean island when they were exiled because of the involvement of Marcus Querini in the Tiepolo conspiracy against the Venetian government in 1310.

The handsome family palazzo in Venice was the setting for many beautiful parties, such as the one given to celebrate the wedding of a Querini girl to Francesco Mocenigo in 1525. There was such excitement and anticipation that members of the aristocratic Valorosi fraternity wore only scarlet red for the week before the gala.

Giovanni, the last Querini-Stampalia, was very interested in science and established a science academy. When he died in 1869 he left the palazzo and its contents—a distinguished collection of paintings and an extensive library—as a foundation. It was a great gift to the city of Venice.

Visitors to the Foundation now have the added pleasure of experiencing an architectural expression of Carlo Scarpa, the much respected Venetian designer, who created a new entrance, ground floor, and garden. His work, begun in 1961, links the venerable palazzo and its treasured contents to the twentieth century. The entrance, an arched bridge over a canal, is a stylized version of a Venetian bridge, a romantic symbol of the city's connection of water and land. The entrance, exhibition, and conference halls are sculpted spaces of marble, stone, metal, and glass, the materials of the region combined and shaped with the hand of this modern poet-artist.

The small garden, enclosed by high walls, has all the elements of a grand garden, and creates a landscape of drama and dimension for the palazzo. Water, sky, and green are brought together in harmony. Stone steps rise to a promenade level; stepping stones lead around the perimeter. Climbing vines, shrubs, and trees are pruned in pleasing shapes. Stone artifacts and a sculpted wall with golden tiles entertain the eye. A reflecting pool brings the sky down to earth. It is the garden of Venice perfected.

In the garden at the Querini-Stampalia Foundation, papyrus and lilies in a water channel are reminiscent of the water gardens of Islam. In an interview with Barbara Radice in Modo, *Carlo Scarpa, the garden's designer, said: "I am Byzantine. I was born near the church of San Marco, therefore I love all the Byzantinism, and consequently Islamicism."*

Overleaf: *Steps to the lawn level, the reflecting pool, and the golden tiled wall.*

Second overleaf: *Keeping the world at bay, walls of English ivy thrive in the moist air and soft sun of Venetian nights and days.*

BIBLIOGRAPHY

ANDRIEUX, MAURICE, *Daily Life in Venice at the Time of Casanova,* George Allen and Unwin, London, 1972

CARTWRIGHT, JULIA, *Italian Gardens of the Renaissance,* Charles Scribner's, New York, 1914

COLE, TOBY, ed., *Venice, a Portable Reader,* Frontier Press, New York, 1986

CORYAT, THOMAS, *Coryat's Crudities,* James Maclehouse, Glasglow, 1905

DAMERINI, GINO, *Gardini di Venezia,* Zanichelli, Bologna, 1931; *D'Annunzio e Venezia,* Mondadori, Verona, 1943

D'ANNUNZIO, GABRIELE, *The Flame of Life,* translated from the Italian, introductory essay by Baron Gustavo Tosti, P. F. Collier, New York, 1900

EDEN, F., *A Garden in Venice,* Country Life & George Newnes, London, 1903

ELLIS, WILLIAM ASHTON, ed., *Richard Wagner to Mathilde Wesendonck,* Milford House, Boston, 1971

FONTANA, GIAN JACOPO, *Cento Palazzi di Venezia,* edited by Francesco Roffare, Scarabellin, Venice,1934

GOETHE, J. W., *Italian Journey,* translated by W. H. Auden and Elizabeth Mayer, North Point Press, San Francisco, 1982

HONOUR, HUGH, *The Companion Guide to Venice,* Collins, London, 1965

JAMES, HENRY, *The Turn of the Screw & The Aspern Papers,* introduction by Kenneth B. Murdock, E. P. Dutton, New York, 1960

LAURITZEN, PETER, and Zieicke, Alexander, *Palaces of Venice,* Viking Press, New York, 1978

LORENZETTI, GIULIO, *Venice and its Lagoon,* Edizioni Lint, Trieste, 1980

MCCARTHY, MARY, *Venice Observed,* William Heinemann, London, 1961

MORRIS, JAMES, *Venice,* Faber and Faber, London, 1960

NAKAMURA, TOSHIO, ed., *Carlo Scarpa,* Architecture and Urbanism, Tokyo, 1985

NICHOLS, ROSE STANDISH, *Italian Pleasure Gardens,* Dodd, Mead, New York, 1931

NORWICH, JOHN JULIUS, *History of Venice,* Viking Press, New York, 1982

RUSKIN, JOHN, *The Stones of Venice,* edited by J. G. Links, Da Capo Press, New York, 1960

SMITH, F. HOPKINSON, *Gondola Days,* Houghton Mifflin, New York, 1897

TASSINI, GIUSEPPE, *Curiosità Veneziane,* edited by Lino Moretti, Filippi, Venice, 1964

VIDAL, GORE, *Vidal in Venice,* Summit Books in association with Antelope, New York, 1985

WHARTON, EDITH, *Italian Villas and their Gardens,* Bodley Head, London, 1904

CREDITS: The drawings reproduced on the pages listed here are from the sources noted.
The authors are thankful for the permission to reproduce these materials:
pp. 50–51: G. Fossati, *View of Venice,* detail, 1743, from Schulz, Juergen, *The Printed Plans and Panoramic Views of Venice,* Leo S. Olski, Florence, 1970.
pp. 96–97: Monastery of Sant'Antonio, detail, Iacopo de'Barbari map, Collection Correr Museum, Venice.
pp. 108–109: Guardi, drawing of the Contarini dal Zaffo garden, Collection Oxford Ashmolean Museum.
pp. 136–137: Luca Carlevaris engraving of Palazzo Zenobio, Collection A. Rubin de Cervin Albrizzi, Venice.
pp. 140–141: Drawing, Zenobio garden plan, Collection A. Rubin de Cervin Albrizzi, Venice.
pp. 158–159: Coronelli, engraving of the Palazzo Soranzo, Colleciton Correr Museum, Venice.
pp. 166–167: G. Borsato, engraving of the Public Garden, Collection Correr Museum, Venice.

INDEX

Overleaf: *Garden of
palazzo Contarini Corfù
dagli Scrigni Rocca*

Second overleaf: *View
from the window of Palazzo
Soranzo Cappello*